When
CHRIST
Appears

When CHRIST Appears

An Inspirational Experience through Revelation

DR. DAVID JEREMIAH

WORTHY®
PUBLISHING

CONTENTS

INTRODUCTION

The book of Revelation promises a special blessing for those who take the time to peer into the future with the apostle John. As you read through its pages, you will see that God wins. Christ triumphs. Righteousness prevails. Satan loses. Sorrow, sickness, and death disappear. A new heaven and earth emerge from the ashes of the old. And God Himself wipes away the tears from every eye. This book fills me with hope, and I hope it does the same for you!

Revelation teaches us that regardless of what happens in this life—no matter how depressing the world news appears or how difficult life becomes—life in Christ has a joyful ending. When the heartache of this present world weighs heavily on us, we have only to look up and look ahead at the radiant end of one story and the joyous beginning of a new story that will never end. It's an eternal story with one central message: "Worthy is the Lamb who was slain" (5:12).

The revelation John received reminds the Church of every age that Jesus Christ is Lord of all; that He will be the ultimate victor over the devil and his representatives; and that He will usher His people into the glorious heavenly city where there will be no more death or despair, nor more pain or suffering. Regardless of the tests and trials that will come upon the earth, this book shows us the final outcome: all things lead to the perfect rule and reign of Christ. This should encourage you to follow Christ no matter the cost and to exchange the world's offerings for Christ's eternal kingdom.

Not everything in the Bible is meant to be crystal clear. For example, many of the wise sayings of Proverbs, as well as the parables of Jesus, demand a search for their meaning. Apocalyptic visions are the same. Reading the book of Revelation requires having ears to hear (2:7, 11, 17, 29; 3:6, 13, 22)—ears that are ready to listen and eager to discover new insights in the details of every sign and symbol.

The central theme of the book of Revelation is worship. It contains glorious scenes of all of heaven worshiping God and the Lamb because they alone are worthy. The central plotline of Revelation is spiritual warfare—Satan, his demons, and his earthly representatives war against the authority of God and His Son. And the central hope of the book—the return of the victorious King—is the ultimate message that God wins the spiritual war.

I invite you to read through Revelation with me. We will explore each verse, gleaning the truthful lessons John left behind after receiving this vision. If you are confident, like I am, that our Lord Jesus Christ will return one day, then we must be prepared for what is to come. Revelation is not fiction—it is an outline of our future. Fear of the future can be debilitating, but rest-assured, Jesus spoke of the future often, and He did so without fear. He faced the future with peace, and so can we as we read His inspired Word.

REVELATION 1:1–3

The revelation from Jesus Christ, which God gave him to show his servants what must soon take place. He made it known by sending his angel to his servant John, who testifies to everything he saw—that is, the word of God and the testimony of Jesus Christ. Blessed is the one who reads aloud the words of this prophecy, and blessed are those who hear it and take to heart what is written in it, because the time is near.

1

UNRAVELING THE MYSTERY

(Revelation 1:1–3)

Many people think of the book of Revelation as an enigma, a mystery, a puzzle to solve—or a puzzle that can't be solved! But the word *revelation* is a translation of the Greek word *apokalupsis*, which means "to reveal, to disclose, to uncover."

The purpose of Revelation is not to conceal but to reveal. The message in the book of Revelation seeks to more fully reveal Jesus Christ to us, to show us who He truly is, in all His glory. The book of Revelation is written both *about* Jesus and *by* Jesus. It tells us that He is coming again, how He is coming, and what condition the world will be in when He comes. It unveils the Lord Jesus Christ as the sovereign King, ruler over all the earth.

It also describes the unfolding of history and the end of the world as we know it. There have always been stories, prophecies, rumors, and questions about "the end." Revelation gives us answers.

In verse 1, John says this book will reveal the events that "must soon take place." This phrase describes an event that will occur suddenly, but not necessarily in the near future. In other words, the events of Revelation may not occur today or tomorrow—but once they do begin to unfold, they will progress in rapid succession.

It's interesting to note that Revelation is the only book in the Bible that promises a blessing to those who read it.

In fact, there are seven distinct blessings in the book:

- "Blessed is the one who reads aloud the words of this prophecy, and blessed are those who hear it and take to heart what is written in it, because the time is near" (1:3).
- "Blessed are the dead who die in the Lord from now on" (14:13).
- "Blessed is the one who stays awake and remains clothed (alert and spiritually prepared), so as not to go naked (spiritually unprepared) and be shamefully exposed" (16:15, parenthetical added).
- "Blessed are those who are invited to the wedding supper of the Lamb" (19:9)!
- "Blessed and holy are those who share in the first resurrection. The second death has no power over them, but they will be priests of God and of Christ and will reign with Him for a thousand years" (20:6).

- "Blessed is the one who keeps the words of the prophecy written in this scroll" (22:7).
- "Blessed are those who wash their robes, that they may have the right to the tree of life and may go through the gates into the city" (22:14).

You can be blessed just by reading Revelation, but the greatest blessing comes when you obey it. The road to true success is found in submitting ourselves to the Word of God and its life-transforming power (Luke 11:28).

Lord, help me to be faithful to read and apply the message of Revelation. Teach me how to apply its truths and to worship You more fully as I come to know You better and learn about Your plan and purpose for the end times.

Read Revelation 1:1–3 in *The Jeremiah Study Bible*.

REVELATION 1:4–6

John,

To the seven churches in the province of Asia:

Grace and peace to you from him who is, and who was, and who is to come, and from the seven spirits before his throne, and from Jesus Christ, who is the faithful witness, the firstborn from the dead, and the ruler of the kings of the earth.

To him who loves us and has freed us from our sins by his blood, and has made us to be a kingdom and priests to serve his God and Father—to him be glory and power for ever and ever! Amen.

2

THE RETURN OF
THE KING
(Revelation 1:4–8)

Ever since Jesus disappeared in the clouds (Acts 1:9), true believers have been looking and longing for His return.

There are two primary purposes of the book of Revelation: to describe the triumphant return of the King and to detail His victorious rule over the kingdom. The apostle John sent this letter to seven churches in Asia, which represented the physical churches of John's day in that area and continues to represent the Church throughout history.

Persecuted believers throughout the Roman Empire would have been especially encouraged to learn that the Savior who was pierced for their transgressions—the One who bore the suffering and shame of death on a cross—would be coming back as King over all the earth, even over the emperor of Rome!

The word *coming* in Revelation 1:7 is the Greek word *parousia*. It not only describes the King's arrival but the profound changes that His arrival produces (Zechariah 12:10–13:6). When I was in school, whenever my teacher stepped away from the classroom, an eraser fight would erupt. Chalky missiles would spread dust all over the room until she returned. Her arrival into the classroom would be a *parousia*. Erasers would drop, and students would become models of good behavior! In a similar way, Jesus's *parousia* will significantly affect the affairs of the world.

When Moses was given the Law by God, a cloud surrounded Mount Sinai (Exodus 19:16). Daniel said that the Messiah would "come with the clouds" (Daniel 7:13). At the Transfiguration, Jesus and His closest disciples were overshadowed by a cloud (Matthew 17:5). And when Jesus ascended to heaven, a cloud received Him (Acts 1:9).

In Revelation 1:8, Jesus Christ announces that He is "the Alpha and the Omega." *Alpha* is the first letter of the Greek alphabet (the beginning), and *Omega* is the last letter (the end). Jesus is saying, "I am A to Z, the beginning and the end and everything in between."

Jesus is also greater than the concept of time. He is the One "who is, and who was, and who is to come" (1:8). He preceded the creation of the earth, and He will succeed its re-creation with the new heavens and the new earth.

In addition to revealing that Jesus is boundless and timeless, Revelation tells us that He is more powerful than we can even begin to comprehend. He is "the Almighty" (1:8). He has been appointed by the Father to defeat Satan once and for all, and soon He will return in power and glory to establish His eternal kingdom.

All believers should study this wonderful book with great excitement and eager anticipation of Jesus's triumphant return!

King Jesus, I worship You as the Alpha and the Omega, the beginning and the end, Lord and ruler of all things—including my life today. Fill me with joyful excitement as I look forward to Your glorious appearing!

Read Revelation 1:4–8 in *The Jeremiah Study Bible*.

REVELATION 1:9–11

I, John, your brother and companion in the suffering and kingdom and patient endurance that are ours in Jesus, was on the island of Patmos because of the word of God and the testimony of Jesus. On the Lord's Day I was in the Spirit, and I heard behind me a loud voice like a trumpet, which said: "Write on a scroll what you see and send it to the seven churches: to Ephesus, Smyrna, Pergamum, Thyatira, Sardis, Philadelphia and Laodicea."

3

THE SUFFERING
SCRIBE

(Revelation 1:9–11)

John had been a leader in the early church as well as a bold and powerful witness for Jesus among Roman believers. As a result, the emperor Domitian, who feared for the control of his empire, forced John into exile on the island of Patmos in the Aegean Sea. That's where he received his visions and wrote the book of Revelation.

John described himself as a "companion in the suffering and kingdom and patient endurance that are ours in Jesus" (1:9). He was not the only biblical writer who experienced hardship and suffering. Think of Moses in the wilderness, David fleeing from Saul, Isaiah being persecuted by kings, and Paul in all sorts of trials.

The apostle John had every right to bemoan his fate—after all, he was the "disciple whom Jesus loved" (John 13:23). He had a track record of great sacrifice, unwavering loyalty, and loving service to the cause of Christ. Yet despite all of this, John was forced into exile in his last years, far removed from everyone and everything he loved. The now-elderly apostle could have moaned, "What did I do to deserve this?" Yet John understood an essential truth about life as a believer in Jesus Christ: we can endure because God is at work, establishing His kingdom for us and through us. His kingdom will prevail!

So many of us cry, "Why me?" when we face problems. But our question *should* be, "Why not me?" Consider: Why should we alone be exempt from trials and suffering? And how might God want to use our pain for His greater purposes?

Alone on the island, when John yielded himself to the Lord, he saw a vision of such majesty that he passed out! You and I probably would have too.

Artists through the centuries have tried to depict the physical appearance of Jesus. But even if we could create an accurate representation of what Jesus looked like when He walked the earth as a man, that appearance is nothing like what John saw on Patmos. When Jesus appeared to John there, He did not appear as the rugged man who walked the hills of Judea. He appeared as the risen, exalted, and glorified Christ who will one day return to establish His eternal kingdom here on earth.

When John had the unique experience of being "in the Spirit" (1:10), the physical limits of time and space were temporarily set aside. In the spirit realm, he was able to move *upward* to see things in heaven and also *forward* in time to see things that would happen in the future.

John received instructions to write the vision and send it to "the seven churches" (1:11). These seven churches—which represent all churches—are pictured as lampstands. When Jesus walked the earth, He was the "light of the world" (John 8:12).

Now that Christ has returned to heaven, believers are responsible for shining His light into the darkness until He comes again (Matthew 5:14).

Jesus, when I encounter trials, give me the grace to ask: "Why not me?" Let me shine Your light even in my suffering. Help me celebrate that no matter what happens to me or how I feel about it, I can be certain that You are faithfully at work, establishing Your kingdom for me, in me, and through me.

Read Revelation 1:9–11 in *The Jeremiah Study Bible*.

REVELATION 1:13–16

And among the lampstands was someone like a son of man, dressed in a robe reaching down to his feet and with a golden sash around his chest. The hair on his head was white like wool, as white as snow, and his eyes were like blazing fire. His feet were like bronze glowing in a furnace, and his voice was like the sound of rushing waters. In his right hand he held seven stars, and coming out of his mouth was a sharp, double-edged sword. His face was like the sun shining in all its brilliance.

4

WHAT "AWESOME" REALLY LOOKS LIKE

(Revelation 1:12–20)

In our churches, we often sing choruses about how "awesome" God is, but John was able to see this awesomeness up close. On the Isle of Patmos, he received a revelation, a vision of glory. There among the seven golden lampstands, the risen Jesus stood before him, "son of man"—deity in human form.

As John describes Jesus's appearance, we discover that each physical aspect is in some way symbolic of His character. His long, flowing robe speaks of His greatness (Isaiah 6:1). The golden sash across His chest speaks of His faithfulness and righteousness (Isaiah 11:5). On one occasion Jesus had appeared with a towel and, as a servant, he had washed His disciples' feet (John 13:4–5). Now He is dressed in majesty, in the glorious splendor of a King.

His hair, "white as snow" (Revelation 1:14), is not a sign of advanced age but absolute holiness and wisdom. It symbolizes the purity of His righteous judgment (Daniel 7:9–13).

John had seen Jesus's eyes filled with compassion,

even tears, while on earth. But now His eyes are like fire, penetrating to the deepest part of the soul. Nothing in all creation is hidden from His gaze (Hebrews 4:13).

His feet "like bronze" speak of the day when Jesus will crush all of His enemies (1 Corinthians 15:24–25). His mighty voice thunders like the roar of many waters. His weapon of warfare is the two-edged sword that proceeds from His mouth. This is the Word of God, which He will use to judge the nations (Hebrews 4:12).

John had seen Jesus on the Mount of Transfiguration (Matthew 17:2); His face now appears as it did that day, shining like the sun "in all its brilliance" (Revelation 1:16). And now, John is overcome—paralyzed by holy fear and reverence. He falls at the feet of Jesus "as though dead" (1:17).

One day we, too, will stand before Jesus and see Him face-to-face (1 Corinthians 13:12). We, too, will fall on our faces before Him—overwhelmed by His awesome power, His holiness, His beauty, and His majesty.

In that day, our victorious King will comfort us— just as He comforts John by placing His right hand on him when he is on his face before Him (1:17). In the Bible, the right hand of God is the hand of salvation; it's His offer of rescue, refuge, and protection. The right hand is the hand of blessing and favor. It's the hand of fellowship.

To John—and to us—Jesus says, "Do not be afraid!"

He is alive, now and forever, raised from the dead in power and glory. He has triumphed over evil, triumphed over the power of sin and death.

Because He lives, and because we are His, we have nothing to fear. *Ever.*

How "awesome" is that?

Lord Jesus, I worship You as the Holy One, the King of kings and Lord of lords, Righteous Judge and ruler over all the earth. You are my Savior and my Friend. How I long for the day of Your appearing!

Read Revelation 1:12–20 in *The Jeremiah Study Bible.*

REVELATION 2:1–4

"*To the angel of the church in Ephesus write:*

These are the words of him who holds the seven stars in his right hand and walks among the seven golden lampstands. I know your deeds, your hard work and your perseverance. I know that you cannot tolerate wicked people, that you have tested those who claim to be apostles but are not, and have found them false. You have persevered and have endured hardships for my name, and have not grown weary.

Yet I hold this against you: You have forsaken the love you had at first."

5

HOW TO LOSE YOUR FIRST LOVE

(Revelation 2:1–4)

Ephesus was once a famous and flourishing Greek city. The apostle Paul founded the church in Ephesus and spent three years discipling the first believers there. He later wrote them the letter we know as the book of Ephesians and established Timothy as their pastor. Many believe that John became their pastor after Timothy, and that he was probably living in Ephesus when he was taken captive and exiled to Patmos.

In Revelation 2, John recorded the first of Jesus's letters to the seven churches in Roman Asia Minor, and he began with a message to the church in Ephesus.

Jesus reminded the Ephesians that He "walks among the seven golden lampstands"—in other words, He was always with them, and He had the power to supply all their needs (2:1). But His presence also meant He was aware of their shortcomings.

Before He dealt with their faults, Christ praised the Ephesian church for what they were doing right. He commended them for their "deeds" and "hard work" (2:2).

Christians today often de-emphasize the importance of works because we don't want to diminish the priority of grace in salvation. But wherever a clear message of grace is preached, you'll find an active, dynamic church, like the church in Ephesus.

In addition, this body of believers was a *disciplined* and *discerning church*. They didn't "tolerate wicked people," ignoring willful sin or excusing evil behavior (2:2). They fought hard to remain pure in doctrine as well. They "tested those who claim to be apostles but are not" and "found them false" (2:2).

Ephesus was also a persevering, enduring, *determined church*. They refused to give up, even as they suffered for the sake of the gospel.

So what could Jesus possibly have had against them?

In all their hard work and busyness on His behalf, they had let their hearts grow cold.

The believers in Ephesus had forsaken their first love for Jesus (Revelation 2:4). They'd forgotten the fervent, personal love they once felt toward Him.

As new believers, most of us are pretty passionate and uninhibited in our expression of love toward Christ and our fellow Christians, as well as in our loving concern for the lost.

However, our passion can fade over time—and good works can become a substitute for a real relationship with Christ. If we're not careful, we'll find ourselves simply going through the motions, acting out of duty, obligation, or even habit, instead of devotion.

We may suppose that as long as—ultimately—we're *doing* all the right things, the attitude of our hearts doesn't really matter. But in those times, Jesus says to us what He said to the Ephesians:

"Consider how far you have fallen! Repent" (2:5).

Lord Jesus, forgive me for the times I've forsaken my first love for You. Show me where my heart has grown cold and rekindle the fire within me. Remind me to put our relationship first, even above all the things I do in Your name or on Your behalf.

Read Revelation 2:1–4 in *The Jeremiah Study Bible.*

REVELATION 2:5–7

Consider how far you have fallen! Repent and do the things you did at first. If you do not repent, I will come to you and remove your lampstand from its place. But you have this in your favor: You hate the practices of the Nicolaitans, which I also hate.

Whoever has ears, let them hear what the Spirit says to the churches. To the one who is victorious, I will give the right to eat from the tree of life, which is in the paradise of God.

6

HOW TO RECOVER YOUR FIRST LOVE

(Revelation 2:5–7)

In his letter to the Ephesians, the apostle Paul commended the church of Ephesus as "God's holy people . . . the faithful" and those "who love our Lord Jesus Christ with an undying love" (Ephesians 1:1, 6:24). Three decades later, when the apostle John wrote to the same church, the believers in Ephesus were still active in service, patient in trial, and steadfast in truth.

But their love for Jesus had grown cold.

In the book of Revelation, Jesus makes it clear that He won't settle for a loveless relationship with us. He has no interest in disciples who are only all duty and obligation.

More than anything else, He wants our hearts. He desires our wholehearted love and devotion (Matthew 22:37).

Jesus gave the church in Ephesus—and all believers who have forsaken their first love—three steps, or exhortations, that would bring them restoration and renewal:

1. *Remember.* Restoration begins with remembering (2:4). We remember why we gave our

hearts to Christ in the first place and what our relationship with Him was like when we were first saved. How excited, enthusiastic, and grateful we felt! We recall how we used to delight in reading His Word, worshiping Him, fellowshipping with other believers, and being His witnesses. We reflect on what it was like when we learned to trust Him with both the simplest and greatest of our needs.

2. *Repent.* To repent means to change our minds and go in the opposite direction (2:5). If we find that we have forsaken our first love, then we make the deliberate choice to change direction and turn back toward Him. We turn our hearts and our minds—and anything else that needs turning, anything else that needs reorienting— back to Him. It's a conscious decision, an act of the will!

3. *Repeat.* We do again the things we did at first (2:5). We practice again and again the faithful steps of discipleship that we once took eagerly and voluntarily as new believers. We make a point of reconnecting with Him, rebuilding the relationship the same way lovers and friends do. We engage in those activities that used to bring us close to Christ and bring us joy. We spend time alone in His presence; we talk openly and honestly with Him; we listen to Him.

If we will make a point of consistently nurturing our relationship with Christ, we can trust that the feelings will return. Our love for Him will be renewed and restored.

In fact, it'll come back stronger, richer, and deeper than ever before.

Lord Jesus, I offer You my heart once more today. Help me remember the joy of my salvation and repent of the ways I've grown increasingly distracted and disconnected from You. Forgive me, Jesus. Remind me of the things I did at first and empower me to do them eagerly once more, as I return to You, the One who first loved me and gave Himself for me.

Read Revelation 2:5–7 in *The Jeremiah Study Bible.*

REVELATION 2:8–10

"To the angel of the church in Smyrna write:

These are the words of him who is the First and the Last, who died and came to life again. I know your afflictions and your poverty—yet you are rich! I know about the slander of those who say they are Jews and are not, but are a synagogue of Satan. Do not be afraid of what you are about to suffer. I tell you, the devil will put some of you in prison to test you, and you will suffer persecution for ten days. Be faithful, even to the point of death, and I will give you life as your victor's crown."

7

AN ETERNAL PERSPECTIVE

(Revelation 2:8–11)

Imagine knowing that at any moment you could lose your job, your home, your reputation, your freedom, your family—even your life—because of your testimony for Christ.

For the church at Smyrna, this kind of persecution was a way of life. When the book of Revelation was written, people who refused to worship Caesar were considered traitors to Rome. As a result, Christians were tortured, boiled in oil, or fed to wild beasts—all for the entertainment of "true" citizens of Rome.

Jesus told the Christians in Smyrna that He knew of their "afflictions" (2:9). They were under unrelenting pressure from the Roman Empire to abandon their faith and conform to the culture.

Jesus also assured these believers He knew of their "poverty" (2:9). Some were robbed by their neighbors with impunity or had their property confiscated by the government. Others were unable to do business and practice their trades all because they refused to worship the Roman emperor.

Jesus said that He knew of the "slander of those who say they are Jews and are not, but are a synagogue of Satan" (2:9). This new cult had added Christianity to their Jewish faith, along with other religious practices. Mixing religions was common in the Roman Empire, as long as the priority of worship was given to the emperor. The synagogue of Satan was actively working to destroy the reputation of the true Church in order to gain followers of their own.

Jesus gave two commandments to the desperately persecuted church at Smyrna: *be fearless* and *be faithful.* "Do not be afraid of what you are about to suffer" and "Be faithful, even to the point of death" (2:10).

Ever since the time of Christ, believers all over the world have experienced great pain and suffering from persecution. Why should we be faithful and fearless until the end? Jesus gives us five reasons:

1. *The reputation of Christ is better than the reputation of any empire or government.* Empires rise and fall. We have put our trust in the One who transcends time and space, and who is more powerful than even death. He is called Faithful and True.

2. *The recognition of Christ is better than the recognition of any empire or government.* His approval is all that matters. We live to hear Him

say to us when we reach heaven, "Well done, good and faithful servant!" (Matthew 25:21).

3. *The riches of Christ are better than the riches of the world.* Like the believers in Smyrna, we are rich in His mercy, His love, His peace, His joy, His salvation, His forgiveness, His fellowship, His provision, His comfort . . . and much more.

4. *The rewards of Christ far outweigh any suffering experienced on earth.* As painful as it is, our suffering is "light and momentary" compared to the eternal and everlasting glory that awaits us as believers in heaven (2 Corinthians 4:17).

5. *The rewards of Christ are better than the rewards of this earth.* Jesus promised rewards that will last forever and can never be taken from us, including the crown of life (Revelation 2:10).

Jesus, when persecution comes, help me keep this eternal perspective. Teach me to focus on You and remember that the blessing of knowing You is better than anything this world has to offer. Make me fearless and faithful to the end.

Read Revelation 2:8–11 in *The Jeremiah Study Bible.*

REVELATION 2:12–16

"*To the angel of the church in Pergamum write:*

These are the words of him who has the sharp, double-edged sword. I know where you live—where Satan has his throne. Yet you remain true to my name. You did not renounce your faith in me, not even in the days of Antipas, my faithful witness, who was put to death in your city—where Satan lives.

Nevertheless, I have a few things against you: There are some among you who hold to the teaching of Balaam. . . . Likewise, you also have those who hold to the teaching of the Nicolaitans. Repent therefore! Otherwise, I will soon come to you and will fight against them with the sword of my mouth.

8

SATAN'S CITY

(Revelation 2:12–17)

Nevada's "Sin City" has nothing on ancient Pergamum. It was once known as "Satan's City"—in the "where Satan has his throne," the place "where Satan lives" (2:13).

To the Christians (yes, there were some!) living in Pergamum, Jesus was described as "him who has the sharp, double-edged sword" (2:12). The Judge of all the earth was standing at their door, ready to deal righteously with the city and all of its inhabitants.

Jesus knew the *circumstances of their faith*. He understood the spiritual darkness that surrounded them, the pressures they faced, and the oppression they experienced living in this wicked city.

Second, Jesus knew the *conviction of their faith*. The Christians in Pergamum had been persecuted and threatened, yet they held fast. They refused to back down or back away from the faith they professed.

Third, Jesus knew the *courage of their faith*. They had been courageous even to the point of martyrdom (2:13). They were bold and determined.

Jesus also knew something else about the church in

Pergamum—something that threatened their spiritual life: Jesus knew the *compromise of their faith*. Some of the believers in Pergamum had given in to the pressure to adopt certain sinful practices of the city. Their lifestyles were not dissimilar from those of the ungodly culture around them.

This same worldly spirit within some churches today makes it difficult to distinguish between the actions of Christians and non-Christians. Believers are called to be holy, which means "different" or "separate."

> For you were once darkness, but now you are light in the Lord. Live as children of light . . . and find out what pleases the Lord. Have nothing to do with the fruitless deeds of darkness, but rather expose them. It is shameful even to mention what the disobedient do in secret. But everything exposed by the light becomes visible—and everything that is illuminated becomes a light. (Ephesians 5:8–13)

Jesus warned the Christians in Pergamum that if they did not separate themselves, they would get caught up in the judgment He was about to execute on the wicked: "Repent therefore! Otherwise, I will soon come to you and will fight against them with the sword of my mouth" (Revelation 2:16).

To those who would heed His call and come out from among Pergamum's pagan peoples, Christ made two promises: He would give them hidden manna and He would give them a white stone with a new name.

When Israel had no food in the desert, God provided manna—bread that fell from heaven (Exodus 16:11–15). In the New Testament, we learn that Jesus Himself is our provision—the Bread of Heaven or "living bread" (John 6:51).

The white stone is a symbol of changeless purity. In the ancient world, such a stone could signify a court verdict of "not guilty" or an "all-access pass" that guaranteed freedom from future imprisonment. Here, it is also a sign of the King's favor.

The lesson for us today is to never underestimate the dangers of compromising our faith—or the rewards of faithfulness.

King Jesus, search my heart today. Show me any ways that I'm compromising my faith with things of this world. Help me walk in purity and remain faithful in times of temptation.

Read Revelation 2:12–17 in *The Jeremiah Study Bible*.

REVELATION 2:18–20

"*To the angel of the church in Thyatira write:*

These are the words of the Son of God, whose eyes are like blazing fire and whose feet are like burnished bronze. I know your deeds, your love and faith, your service and perseverance, and that you are now doing more than you did at first.

Nevertheless, I have this against you: You tolerate that woman Jezebel, who calls herself a prophet. By her teaching she misleads my servants into sexual immorality and the eating of food sacrificed to idols.

9

A POLLUTED WITNESS
(Revelation 2:18–29)

Sometimes "good" just isn't good enough. Ask the church at Thyatira. They receive a commendation from Jesus for their good "deeds," "love," "faith," "service," and "perseverance" (2:19). This was a church that worked hard and held on to their hope in Christ through trying circumstances. But in Revelation 2, we learn that their failure in one major area had overshadowed all the good they have done.

It seems the church at Thyatira had everything but holiness. Recall the practices of Queen Jezebel from 1 and 2 Kings. When she married Ahab, Jezebel brought her pagan religion to Israel—and with it, every kind of immorality, idolatry, and corruption. Apparently there was a woman in the church of Thyatira who, like Jezebel, was promoting wickedness and idolatry, encouraging believers to indulge in evil and immoral practices like "sexual immorality and the eating of food sacrificed to idols" (Revelation 2:20).

The Lord gave His message to this church in three parts. One part was addressed to the cult of Jezebel, the woman in Thyatira and her followers (2:21–23).

The second part was addressed to the Christians in the church (2:24–25). A final word was added for those who would be victorious (2:26–29).

First, the Lord promised to transform Jezebel's bed, where she had committed her sin, into a place of pain. Christ had given those in the Jezebel cult time to repent, but they had refused. As a result, He warned that judgment would come so that all the churches would know that He was not deceived by outward displays of righteousness (those good deeds). He saw what was done in secret; He is the One who searches the minds and hearts of believers.

Second, Jesus gave a message to the Christians who had not followed after Jezebel. He saw how weary and overwhelmed they were and spared them from any additional burden. In our day, we tend to multiply rules in the body of Christ, but here, Jesus simply says, "Just serve God and keep doing what you are doing."

Finally, Jesus gave a word to "the one who is victorious and does my will to the end" (2:26). Everyone who fights to hold on to holy obedience will be given a position of judgment over the nations (1 Corinthians 6:2). This refers to the Millennium, when the saints will reign with Christ. The overcomers were also given the promise of the morning star, Jesus Christ (Revelation 22:16). This is the promise of the Rapture, when Christ will return for His Church before the dark hours of the Tribulation.

Jesus called those ensnared in the immorality of those around them to repent of their compromise, which had polluted their witness. If they had resisted temptation thus far, then they were to remain steadfast in their commitment to purity and faithful obedience.

In today's culture, His Word holds renewed urgency: "Whoever has ears, let them hear what the Spirit says to the churches" (2:29).

Lord Jesus, show me any area of my heart or life that has been polluted by the evil influences of the world around me. Cleanse me and create in me a new heart, one committed to holiness and faithfulness to You.

Read Revelation 2:18–29 in *The Jeremiah Study Bible.*

REVELATION 3:1–3

"To the angel of the church in Sardis write:

These are the words of him who holds the seven spirits of God and the seven stars. I know your deeds; you have a reputation of being alive, but you are dead. Wake up! Strengthen what remains and is about to die, for I have found your deeds unfinished in the sight of my God. Remember, therefore, what you have received and heard; hold it fast, and repent. But if you do not wake up, I will come like a thief, and you will not know at what time I will come to you.

10

THE CHURCH OF
THE LIVING DEAD

(Revelation 3:1–6)

Y ou know you've got a problem when Jesus doesn't have anything good to say about you.

For the church in Smyrna, the Lord had only praise. For the churches of Ephesus, Pergamum, and Thyatira, He had some words of praise, along with correction. But for the church at Sardis, it was all bad news. He began, "I know your deeds; you have a reputation of being alive, but you are dead" (3:1).

To others, they might appear to be healthy and flourishing, but He knew their heart's true condition. If they wanted to survive—or revive their spiritual lives— Jesus told them to do five essential things:

First, He told the church to *be vigilant.* "Wake up!" (3:2). Christ called the church to keep watch like a sentry responsible for the safety of an army. Situated atop a mountain, the city of Sardis was surrounded by cliffs on three sides and a narrow isthmus on the fourth— causing the people to be overconfident in their security. Years before, Sardis had been conquered by a surprise attack, which may have prompted Jesus's warning to the church to be watchful regarding their spiritual state.

Second, Jesus told the church to *be vigorous*. He said, "Strengthen what remains" (3:2). The faithful Christians in Sardis—the tiny remnant through which the light of Christ remained alive—needed to be strengthened and built up. Although this church was near death, a few of its members had not "soiled their clothes" with sin and compromise and would be "dressed in white" (3:5), their robes representing their righteousness in Christ.

Third, Jesus told the church to *be victorious*. They needed to finish what they had started. "Do you not know that in a race all the runners run, but only one gets the prize? Run in such a way as to get the prize" (1 Corinthians 9:24).

Fourth, Jesus told the church to *be vibrant*. Speaking of the teaching that they had heard and received, He said, "Hold it fast" (Revelation 3:3). He was calling them to live in active obedience to the Word of God.

Finally, Jesus told the church to *be virtuous*. He said, "Repent" (3:3):

> Therefore, with minds that are alert and fully sober, set your hope on the grace to be brought to you when Jesus Christ is revealed at his coming. As obedient children, do not conform to the evil desires you had when you lived in

ignorance. But just as he who called you is holy, so be holy in all you do; for it is written: "Be holy, because I am holy." (1 Peter 1:13–16)

To the faithful in Sardis, the Lord promised He would never erase their names from the "book of life" (Revelation 3:5).

As Christians, we cannot lose our salvation, but our lives can so grieve the Holy Spirit that they have no power or vibrancy. And when many or most of the people in a church live this way, then the church has become dead to the things of the Lord. As the individual members go, so goes the church.

Lord, You know the true condition of my heart. Help me commit to hold fast to Your Word, and live today—and every day—victoriously, with vigilance, virtue, and vibrancy.

Read Revelation 3:1–6 in *The Jeremiah Study Bible.*

REVELATION 3:7–10

"To the angel of the church in Philadelphia write:

These are the words of him who is holy and true, who holds the key of David. What he opens no one can shut, and what he shuts no one can open. I know your deeds. See, I have placed before you an open door that no one can shut. I know that you have little strength, yet you have kept my word and have not denied my name. I will make those who are of the synagogue of Satan, who claim to be Jews though they are not, but are liars—I will make them come and fall down at your feet and acknowledge that I have loved you. Since you have kept my command to endure patiently, I will also keep you from the hour of trial that is going to come on the whole world to test the inhabitants of the earth."

11

A CALL TO COURAGE

(Revelation 3:7–13)

What does it take to please Jesus? The church in Philadelphia is a beautiful example. Here are the words of appreciation, commendation, and encouragement the Savior spoke to them:

First, Jesus told the church in Philadelphia, "I have placed before you an open door that no one can shut" (3:8). An open door in Scripture is an opportunity for ministry (1 Corinthians 16:8–9). It's reassuring to know that Christ is the One opens doors to ministry, and the doors He opens, no one else can shut. He is the One who prepares hearts to receive the gospel; He blesses and prospers the work of His Word, causing it to flourish and be fruitful.

Second, when Jesus said to the church, "you have little strength" (Revelation 3:8), it was meant as a commendation, not a complaint. They knew they were completely dependent on Him for the power to walk in obedience and love—and that's as it should be!

Jesus was also pleased that they keep God's Word (Revelation 3:8). Surrounded by pagan cultures, customs, and influences, the church at Philadelphia had the courage to open their hearts to the Truth. They had heard the Word of God, they had received it, and they believed it. And now they remained faithful to it.

Finally, Jesus commended the church of Philadelphia because they did not deny His name. In the first century there was much controversy about the deity of Christ. But the church at Philadelphia stood strong in their belief that Jesus is God in the flesh.

Jesus made a promise to the church that had great prophetic significance. He told them that He would keep them from "the hour of trial" that would come on the whole world (3:10). Notice that He did not say, "I will also keep you *through* the hour of trial" but rather, "I will also keep you *from* the hour of trial." Jesus was talking about the Rapture. He promised that this church would be taken up into heaven and spared the terrors of the "hour of trial"—the Tribulation.

The Lord told the church to be ready, for "I am coming soon" (3:11). He urged them to keep holding on to their faith so that no one could take away their crown (their reward). The New Jerusalem will be their destination if they persevere in their loyalty and faithfulness to Him.

Where there are Philadelphian Christians, you'll find people excited about the open door of ministry. You'll find people who recognize how much God is doing in their church in spite of their "little strength." And,

Philadelphian Christians teach the Word of God faithfully. But all of these commendable traits will produce little fruit unless we have the courage to walk through the doors God has opened for us.

Today, I pray that your church and mine will not only see the doors He has opened for us, but that we will also courageously walk through them to minister to others in His power, for His glory and His name's sake.

Lord Jesus, thank You for Your Word and for Your mighty power at work in me and through me. Help me make the most of every opportunity for ministry that You open to me today.

Read Revelation 3:7–13 in *The Jeremiah Study Bible*.

REVELATION 3:10

Since you have kept my command to endure patiently, I will also keep you from the hour of trial that is going to come on the whole world to test the inhabitants of the earth.

12

READY OR NOT

(Revelation 3:10)

The Rapture of the Church is one of the most fascinating and hotly debated events prophesied to take place in the end times. Interestingly, the word *rapture* doesn't appear in our English Bibles. *Rapture* comes from the Latin word *rapio* ("to snatch away"), which is translated "caught up" in 1 Thessalonians 4:17.

Those who study the Scripture usually hold one of three views on the timing of the Rapture. According to the *pre-tribulation* view, the Rapture of the Church will occur before the Tribulation. The *mid-tribulation* view says that the Rapture will happen at the midpoint—about three and a half years into the Tribulation. The *post-tribulation* view holds the Rapture will occur at the very end of the Tribulation.

There are many reasons to believe in a pre-tribulation Rapture. For example, did you notice that the word *church* appears nineteen times in Revelation 1–3? But from Revelation 4 on, which describes the Tribulation, there is no further reference to the Church on earth. John never mentions the Church's presence anywhere but in heaven. It would seem logical that if we were going to have to experience this terrifying time of trial and tribulation on earth, the Lord would have included some reference to it.

Another indication that the Church is in heaven during the Tribulation is the description of the twenty-four seats around the throne of God (Revelation 4). Many Bible scholars believe the twenty-four elders represent the Church, which is, therefore, in heaven as the Tribulation begins on earth.

Paul taught that the Day of the Lord will not happen until "the one who now holds [lawlessness] back" is taken away (2 Thessalonians 2:7). This refers to the Holy Spirit, who indwells the Church. But as long as the Church is on earth, the Holy Spirit must be present.

Finally, in his vision, John saw Christ coming to earth at the end of the Tribulation. He was accompanied by "the armies of heaven"—also a reference to the Church (Revelation 19:14).

I believe the Rapture and the Second Coming are separated by the seven-year Tribulation. At the Rapture, Christ comes for His Bride, celebrates the "wedding of the Lamb" with her in heaven during the Tribulation (19:7), and then returns with her to earth at His Second Coming.

The purpose of the Rapture, then, is to remove the Church from earth before the wrath of God is unleashed. In 1 Thessalonians 4:17, we have God's promise that the dead in Christ and those still living at the time, will be "caught up together . . . to meet the Lord in the air." These are such words of comfort for all believers.

Though some claim to have figured out when the Rapture will occur with complicated calculations, the Bible tells us no one knows the exact hour or the precise day . . . not even Jesus (Mark 13:32). As a wise person once observed, the point is not to try to figure out *when* but to be ready whenever!

The Rapture of the Church will be a glorious occasion unlike anything in the history of the world. May the Lord find us ready and waiting.

Jesus, thank You for Your mercy and grace! Thank You for saving me from the wrath to come. Help me be ready and waiting for the Rapture—which could happen at any moment!

Read Essentials of the Christian Faith article, "The Rapture" in *The Jeremiah Study Bible,* p. 1842.

REVELATION 3:14–18

"To the angel of the church in Laodicea write:
These are the words of the Amen, the faithful
and true witness, the ruler of God's creation. I
know your deeds, that you are neither cold nor
hot. I wish you were either one or the other! So,
because you are lukewarm—neither hot nor
cold—I am about to spit you out of my mouth.
You say, 'I am rich; I have acquired wealth and
do not need a thing.' But you do not realize that
you are wretched, pitiful, poor, blind and naked.
I counsel you to buy from me gold refined in the
fire, so you can become rich; and white clothes to
wear, so you can cover your shameful nakedness;
and salve to put on your eyes, so you can see."

13

A PRESCRIPTION FOR WELLNESS

(Revelation 3:14–22)

H as anyone ever said to you, or have you ever said to another person, "You make me sick!"? Those are strong words, but it's exactly the message Jesus had for the church at Laodicea.

Laodicea was a wealthy city, known for its advances in business, science, and industry. But Jesus had nothing positive to say about the church in this city.

The Laodicean believers were comfortably proud of their own wealth, their own status, and their own accomplishments "for the kingdom." They thought they were prosperous and successful, but in reality, Jesus said they were "wretched, pitiful, poor, blind and naked" (3:17).

In His letters to the other churches, Jesus was angered by apostasy, but He became positively ill—absolutely disgusted—by the casual indifference of the Laodiceans. He said to the church, "Because you are lukewarm—neither hot nor cold—I am about to spit you out of my mouth" (3:16).

This is the only place in the New Testament where the word *lukewarm* is used. It's actually drawn from the geography of the city. The water at Laodicea was not drinkable, so the city had water pumped in from surrounding cities—hot water from Hierapolis (north) and cold water from Colossae (south). Hot water can be cleansing and healing; cold water can be refreshing. But by the time the water reached Laodicea, it was lukewarm and hard to stomach—just like the faith of the church there.

Unfortunately, there are many Laodicean churches today. They have become lukewarm about the gospel. They have lost their zeal for evangelism; they don't take a stand on spiritual and moral issues.

Some churches grow vast congregations, increase the variety and number of their programs, and build larger and larger buildings to accomplish their purposes—which they mistake for those of Christ. In reality, He may be pushed outside and left knocking at the door. How sad to think of Him returning to His Church at the end of the age and finding Himself *persona non grata*!

In light of their lukewarm condition, Christ, the Great Physician, gave the church at Laodicea—and lukewarm churches today—five prescriptions:

1. For spiritual poverty, Jesus prescribed "gold"—spiritual riches, such as character and virtue, and other blessings and rewards—all refined in the fire of suffering (3:18).

2. For spiritual nakedness, Jesus prescribed the garments of righteousness (3:18).

3. For spiritual blindness, Jesus prescribed a spiritual salve that would open their eyes to their true spiritual condition (3:18).

4. For spiritual compromise, Jesus prescribed repentance and zeal (3:19).

5. For their spiritual deafness, Jesus prescribed a listening ear, to hear His voice—His knock—and open the door and welcome Him to come in (3:20).

What about you? Are you rich in Christ and in Christlike character? Are you growing in the knowledge and in the fullness of His grace (Colossians 1:9–10)?

How have you opened the door of your heart to Him lately?

Lord God, give me a heart that burns with love and holy zeal for You! Forgive me for the times I have been lukewarm. Jesus, I gladly open the door of my heart and welcome You to come in today.

Read Revelation 3:14–22 in *The Jeremiah Study Bible*.

REVELATION 4:1–2

After this I looked, and there before me was a door standing open in heaven. And the voice I had first heard speaking to me like a trumpet said, "Come up here, and I will show you what must take place after this." At once I was in the Spirit, and there before me was a throne in heaven with someone sitting on it.

14

A GLIMPSE OF GLORY
(Revelation 4:1–11)

Suddenly John found himself summoned to appear before the majestic throne of the King of the universe. And like a preview of coming attractions, his vision in Revelation 4 gives us a glimpse of heaven. We get a glimpse of what's going on there, while the Tribulation unfolds here on earth.

John was at a loss to describe the great beauty he witnessed—the magnificent glory of God. All he could do was try to compare it to earth's most precious treasures, rare jewels and gemstones.

An emerald rainbow surrounded the throne, but unlike the arcs we're familiar with, this rainbow was a full circle—a reminder that in heaven all things are complete. Rainbows are also a reminder of God's faithfulness, from the earliest days of Noah and the great flood to the end of days. Just as He rescued Noah and his family from worldwide disaster, He will rescue His Church through the Rapture.

In Revelation 4:4, John also described twenty-four elders dressed in white, crowned in gold, and seated on their own thrones. These saints probably represent the Church before the throne of God.

John said, "From the throne came flashes of lightning, rumblings and peals of thunder" (4:5). When the Lord gave Israel the Law, His presence was accompanied by lightning, thunder, and a voice from heaven (Exodus 20:18). Today, because of Jesus, the throne of judgment has become the throne of grace for believers (Hebrews 4:16).

John also described a "sea of glass, clear as crystal" surrounding God's throne (Revelation 4:6). And around the throne were four living creatures—the same ones Ezekiel saw in his vision of heaven (Ezekiel 1:5–14). These are the angels who will execute judgment on the earth. They also lead worship in heaven.

In the midst of the thunder and lightning and voices, the angels burst forth with shouts of praise: "'Holy, holy, holy is the Lord God Almighty,' who was, and is, and is to come" (Revelation 4:8).

In the presence of God, the elders were overcome with awe, reverence, and adoration. They fell down in worship, casting their crowns before His throne.

In heaven, we will want nothing more than to bless God and give Him all that we are, all that we have. But of course all we'll have to give are the things He has given us—our "crowns," our rewards. So we'll gladly offer them to Him, saying, "You are worthy, our Lord and God, to receive glory and honor and power, for you created all things, and by your will they were created and have their being" (4:11).

In heaven, the Church will experience an intimacy in worship that the angels can't know. It's something only those who have been rescued and redeemed can understand. We were lost and now we are found. We've been forgiven and set free.

We'll worship more fully in heaven, but we can begin to express our gratitude now.

Holy Lord, I worship You today for all that You are and all that You have done! You alone are worthy of all my praise!

Read Revelation 4:1–11 in *The Jeremiah Study Bible.*

REVELATION 5:4–5

I wept and wept because no one was found who was worthy to open the scroll or look inside. Then one of the elders said to me, "Do not weep! See, the Lion of the tribe of Judah, the Root of David, has triumphed. He is able to open the scroll and its seven seals."

15

WHO IS WORTHY?
(Revelation 5:1–6)

A fascinating scene unfolds in heaven. God is seated on His throne, and in His hands He holds a scroll sealed with seven seals (5:1). This scroll is, in essence, the title deed to the earth. I believe the contents are the same as those sealed up by God "until the time of the end," in the vision He gave to the prophet Daniel thousands of years earlier (Daniel 12:9). What was sealed in Daniel's day is now unsealed in John's.

The scroll, which is about to be opened, unfolds the entire history of the Tribulation from the beginning to the end.

An angel asks, "Who is worthy to break the seals and open the scroll?" (Revelation 5:2).

It's a question that causes John to weep. No one in heaven, on earth, or under the earth is noble enough to open the scroll or powerful enough to establish God's kingdom.

Relief comes, however, when John discovers there *is* One who *is* worthy and learns His identity. There are three names given in Scripture for the One who takes the scroll and unfolds its truth:

1. *The Lion of the tribe of Judah* (Genesis 49:8–10). Under the anointing of the Spirit, Jacob prophesied that the Messiah would come from the descendants of his son Judah. King David was a descendant of the tribe of Judah, as was Joseph, Jesus's legal father.

2. *The Root of David* (Isaiah 11:1, 10). Jesus was a descendant of David, and He was also the Root of David. How can Jesus be both the ancestor and descendant of David? In His humanity Jesus is the son of David (Matthew 22:42), and in His deity He is the ancestor of David (John 8:58).

3. *The Passover Lamb who was slain* (Isaiah 52:13–53:12; John 1:29). This title is the most moving for us as believers. First, *the Lamb is standing,* representing the resurrected Christ. Second, *the Lamb is slain.* The marks of Jesus's death will be visible throughout eternity as a reminder of what it cost Him to purchase our redemption. Third, *the Lamb is strong.* The seven horns indicate His strength (Revelation 5:6). Though the Lamb has been slain, He has not been weakened. Fourth, *the Lamb is searching.* The seven eyes represent His all-seeing wisdom, necessary in order to execute a just judgment upon the earth.

A lion and a lamb are a study in contrasts. The Lamb of God was Jesus at His first coming, the Lion of Judah at His second. The Lamb is meek; the Lion is majestic. The Lamb is the Savior; the Lion is the Sovereign. The Lamb was judged; the Lion is the Judge. The Lamb brings the grace of God; the Lion brings the government of God.

All of this and more are wrapped up in the Person who holds—and unfolds—the scroll.

Lord Jesus, I worship You as the Lamb of God and the Lion of Judah. Only You are worthy to unseal the scroll! Today, help me stand in Your grace and walk in faithful obedience to You.

Read Revelation 5:1–6 in *The Jeremiah Study Bible*.

REVELATION 5:13

Then I heard every creature in heaven and on earth and under the earth and on the sea, and all that is in them, saying:

"To him who sits on the throne and to the Lamb

be praise and honor and glory and power,

for ever and ever!"

16

THE ANCIENT OF DAYS
(*Revelation 5:7–14*)

In heaven, joy cannot be contained. Finally, there is One who has been found worthy to break the seals, open the scroll, and take possession of the earth for God's eternal glory! And now praise erupts in the form of a triumphant song celebrating what He has done (providing redemption through His death and resurrection)—and what He is about to do (reclaim His authority over the earth and rule it justly).

Daniel 7:13–14 gives us some background for this scene. There, the prophet had a vision of One "like a son of man" who comes with the clouds and is led into the presence of the Ancient of Days, a title that literally means "the One who has been around forever, the One who never had a beginning." We're told that this son of man will receive "authority, glory and sovereign power." All the nations and peoples of the earth will worship Him—in every land and in every language. Unlike that of earthly kings who rise and fall, His dominion is everlasting; His kingdom will not pass away.

Revelation 5 shows us the fulfillment of this prophecy. Jesus is receiving the kingdom from His Father. At the end of the Tribulation, He will return to earth with full authority to administer justice and judge all who are in rebellion against God. He will take ownership of the earth and establish His reign as King of kings and Lord of lords.

When this happens, three groups in heaven break out into songs of praise and adoration. Notice that the worship broadens in ever-increasing circles. It began with the four living creatures and the twenty-four elders in Revelation 4; here it continues as the angels join in, and then finally every creature lifts its voice!

In Revelation 5:8–10, we see the worship of the *redeemed*. The elders represent the Church, and they praise the Lamb who is worthy because He has redeemed those who will reign with Him on earth. In verses 11–12, we see the worship of *angels*, "thousands upon thousands, and ten thousand times ten thousand." This is an extravagant way of saying a number beyond measure. Can you imagine what such a chorus of angels would sound like? At last, in verse 13, even the *animal kingdom* praises the Lamb.

Whether their praises are sung or spoken, there is no missing the fact that the central focus of heaven during the Tribulation is worship of the Lamb who was slain, in joyous anticipation of the victorious reign He is about to establish on earth—just as He reigns in heaven.

But He won't reign alone.

"If we died with him, we will also live with him; if we endure, we will also reign with him" (2 Timothy 2:11–12). Believers who persevere under trial will be rewarded.

Daniel saw it all unfold in his vision: "The Ancient of Days came and pronounced judgment in favor of the holy people of the Most High, and the time came when they possessed the kingdom" (Daniel 7:22).

Triune God, You are worthy to receive all worship and honor and praise from all creation—including animals, angels, and people—now and forevermore! I worship You in anticipation of the day You will establish Your triumphant reign here on earth. Reign in me today.

Read Revelation 5:7–14 in *The Jeremiah Study Bible.*

I watched as the Lamb opened the first of the seven seals. Then I heard one of the four living creatures say in a voice like thunder, "Come!" I looked, and there before me was a white horse! Its rider held a bow, and he was given a crown, and he rode out as a conqueror bent on conquest.

When the Lamb opened the second seal, I heard the second living creature say, "Come!" Then another horse came out, a fiery red one. Its rider was given power to take peace from the earth and to make people kill each other. To him was given a large sword.

When the Lamb opened the third seal, I heard the third living creature say, "Come!" I looked, and there before me was a black horse! Its rider was holding a pair of scales in his hand. . . .

When the Lamb opened the fourth seal, I heard the voice of the fourth living creature say, "Come!" I looked, and there before me was a pale horse! Its rider was named Death, and Hades was following close behind him.

17

THE FOUR HORSEMEN

(Revelation 6:1–8)

They've become legendary—mythological, in a sense. People who know almost nothing else about the book of Revelation usually know (at least generally) about "The Four Horsemen of the Apocalypse."

More than harbingers of doom, these horses and riders are the agents of God's judgment, actively unleashing His wrath on a wicked and unrepentant world.

In the Old Testament, horses represented war (Zechariah 6:1–8). Here in Revelation 6, the four horses represent God's conquest of the powers of darkness on the earth.

The first rider is on a white horse. In Eastern imagery, a white horse represented a conqueror. This rider is the Antichrist, who arrives at the beginning of the Tribulation as a victorious leader. His bow is a sign of his ability to conquer. He carries no arrows because he subdues the nations in the name of peace. However, it is a false peace. As a great deceiver, the Antichrist will take control of the world without war.

The second rider is on a fiery red horse. This rider personifies war and bloodshed. The assassin's sword in his hand is the kind used to cut the throats of people and animals. The false peace promised by the Antichrist gives way to a time of murder, bloodshed, revolution, and war (Matthew 24:6, 21).

The third rider is on a black horse. In times of war, food is often in short supply. Famine rides behind the horse of war, bringing worldwide starvation.

The fourth rider is on a pale horse, and he has another following him. Death is the rider, with Hades close behind. They are both armed with the "sword, famine and plague" and "the wild beasts of the earth" (Revelation 6:8).

We have seen pestilence and plagues wreak havoc on our world. But Revelation tells us that the greatest epidemic the world has ever known will arise during the Tribulation, resulting in 25 percent of the world's population being killed (6:8).

It's comforting to remember that those who know Jesus Christ as their Lord and Savior will be worshiping Him in heaven while the events of Revelation 6–19 unfold on the earth. Because of Jesus, we don't have to experience God's judgment and wrath. Jesus bore it for us when He died on the cross in our place. It's reason enough for us to spend our days in worship and praise.

But there's another response believers should have to this scene in Revelation. We should feel compassion and grave concern for the lost, especially our loved ones—friends, family, and neighbors who do not yet know Christ. Otherwise, they may very well suffer all the horrors of the Tribulation in the days to come.

A better understanding of Bible prophecy can be one of the greatest motivators for telling others about Jesus Christ.

Lord, fill my heart with respect for Your righteousness, gratitude for Your grace, and confidence in my salvation. Give me the boldness to share Your gospel with those in my life who need to know You too.

Read Revelation 6:1–8 in *The Jeremiah Study Bible.*

REVELATION 6:9–11

When he opened the fifth seal, I saw under the altar the souls of those who had been slain because of the word of God and the testimony they had maintained. They called out in a loud voice, "How long, Sovereign Lord, holy and true, until you judge the inhabitants of the earth and avenge our blood?" Then each of them was given a white robe, and they were told to wait a little longer, until the full number of their fellow servants, their brothers and sisters, were killed just as they had been.

18

THE CRY OF THE MARTYRS

(Revelation 6:9–11)

Today in countries all over the world, millions of Christians are persecuted and denied even the most fundamental human rights. Every year thousands of Christians are martyred for their faith. But nothing the world has ever seen will compare to the grand-scale persecution of Christians that will take place during the calamitous events of the earth's final seven years.

Sometimes we wonder, *How can a loving God cause (or allow) these terrible things to happen?* It's important to remember that according to Scripture, sin entered the earth through Adam and Eve's disobedience to God (Romans 5:12). All of the pain and suffering is a result of that first sin.

Revelation shows us how Jesus Christ will return in power and glory and take back control of the earth forever. He will break the curse and reverse the consequences of our sin. But specific events must occur before that happens. Certain things have to fall into place before He establishes His eternal kingdom. When the

Greatest Story Ever Told reaches its final chapter, there will be no loose ends.

Jesus foretold the persecution that would come (Matthew 24:8–10), and Zechariah the prophet spoke of the Tribulation as a time when two-thirds of the Jewish population would be killed (Zechariah 13:8). But speaking on behalf of God, he also made this promise: "I will refine them like silver and test them like gold. They will call on my name and I will answer them" (Zechariah 13:9).

In heaven, John sees the souls of those who have already been slain "under the altar" (Revelation 6:9). That's where the Old Testament priests poured the blood of the sacrifices (Exodus 29:12). So to be "under the altar" is a symbol of being covered by the blood of Christ. This multitude is saved, under the blood, and protected in heaven.

These martyrs are people who became believers during the Tribulation and remained faithful through intense persecution. They did not give in, back down, or fall for the Antichrist's lies. They were called on to demonstrate their faith—often with their lives. And ultimately, they overcame the enemy.

The martyred Tribulation saints now cry out to God for justice; they call on the Righteous Judge to avenge them (Revelation 6:10).

The Lord's answer to their cry is to give them white robes of righteousness and words of comfort. They are to rest for a while longer and then He will set the balances right once and for all.

As we see throughout Scripture, our sovereign God is always at work—sometimes behind the scenes, sometimes before our eyes. Though we may not always comprehend it, we can rest assured that He has a perfect plan for all of us and all of history, which He will accomplish according to His perfect timing.

God, forgive me for ever thinking You were unjust, uncaring, or unable to help me when I couldn't see You at work in my life right away. I know You are faithful and just, constantly working all things together for my good. Help me trust You and Your timing. And help me patiently bear any suffering or persecution You may call me to endure for Your name's sake.

Read Revelation 6:9–11 in *The Jeremiah Study Bible.*

REVELATION 6:12–14

I watched as he opened the sixth seal. There was a great earthquake. The sun turned black like sackcloth made of goat hair, the whole moon turned blood red, and the stars in the sky fell to earth, as figs drop from a fig tree when shaken by a strong wind. The heavens receded like a scroll being rolled up, and every mountain and island was removed from its place.

19

WHEN THE WHOLE WORLD TREMBLES

(Revelation 6:12–17)

The Scripture tells us that God created us for His glory. He chose to love us and live with us, to connect with us and commune with us. But the inhabitants of the earth are a wayward, stubborn, and rebellious lot. Too often we've spurned His love. We've steadfastly ignored His warning about the dangers of sin and its consequences. Though He has repeatedly offered forgiveness, many have turned their backs on Him completely.

And now the day of reckoning has come—the Day of the Lord—just as He said it would. Accounts must be settled; the penalty for sin must be paid. Those who have refused His grace and mercy will receive His justice.

At the opening of the sixth seal, a great earthquake shakes the whole earth. Then the sun turns black as sackcloth and the moon turns red like blood (6:12). Next, John says that the "stars in the sky fell to earth" (6:13). These "stars" are likely meteors that will pummel the earth.

Some scholars think the earthquake and the asteroids will trigger the earth's crust to slide. The people who live in the regions where the earth's crust is shifting would observe the heavens appearing to move in the opposite direction, which would seem like John's description of "a scroll being rolled up." A continental shift would result in "every mountain and island was removed from its place" (6:14).

Imagine how frightening all of this would be and how it would disrupt every aspect of life as we know it. It is as if God has reached down and is shaking the planet—causing everything to come loose.

There are three lessons we can learn:

First, we see *the horror of sin.* The destruction caused by sin and subsequent judgment is truly horrifying. The excruciating pain and suffering that result are beyond our comprehension.

Second, we see *the hiding of sin.* In their terror, "the kings of the earth, the princes, the generals, the rich, the mighty, and everyone else, both slave and free" will try to hide themselves (6:15). But no one will be exempt from the judgment of God. "Nothing in all creation is hidden from God's sight" (Hebrews 4:13).

Thankfully, those of us who have trusted in Christ don't need to hide because our guilt and shame has been erased. Jesus has already taken the punishment in our place and presents us to God "without stain or wrinkle or any other blemish, but holy and blameless" (Ephesians 5:27).

Third, we see *the hardness of sin*. We would think that when faced with devastation all around them, people would admit that God is God, and fall down on their faces and repent. But sin so hardens the heart that those living in the last days would rather die than repent and be forgiven.

The message for us today is to take seriously the power of sin and its painful consequences. May we continually humble our hearts in repentance and strive to walk daily in faithful obedience to Him.

Lord God, forgive me for my sin. Help me to see it the way You do and be mindful of its effects. Teach me to choose righteousness instead and to live in the light of Your Word.

Read Revelation 6:12–17 in *The Jeremiah Study Bible*.

REVELATION 7:1–4

After this I saw four angels standing at the four corners of the earth, holding back the four winds of the earth to prevent any wind from blowing on the land or on the sea or on any tree. Then I saw another angel coming up from the east, having the seal of the living God. He called out in a loud voice to the four angels who had been given power to harm the land and the sea: "Do not harm the land or the sea or the trees until we put a seal on the foreheads of the servants of our God." Then I heard the number of those who were sealed: 144,000 from all the tribes of Israel.

20

A PROMISE KEPT
(Revelation 7:1–8)

Suddenly John sees four angels restraining the winds of judgment that are about to blow upon the earth in every direction. Until God's chosen ones are safe, the four destructive winds will not be allowed to blow. The elect from Israel must be gathered together.

Like a parenthesis between the sixth and seventh seals, Revelation 7 records two separate visions. The first (7:1–8) reveals the existence and destiny of 144,000 witnesses—Jewish believers—who will survive the Tribulation. The second vision (7:9–17) describes the honor that will be given in heaven to the Gentiles who had been martyred for their faith in Christ.

Many people want to be included in the 144,000, but in this instance, only Jews qualify—twelve thousand descendants from each of Israel's twelve tribes (remember, the Church is already in heaven). These "sealed" witnesses who remain on the earth are servants of God who have not bowed to the Antichrist. The Lord will preserve them through the Tribulation so that they'll be alive when the Millennium begins, thus fulfilling God's covenant promises to His people.

God always keeps His promises.

Throughout the Old Testament, many times and in many places, God promised His people that despite the judgment they incurred, He would not allow them to be completely destroyed. They would never be wiped from the face of the earth. He would always protect and preserve a righteous remnant.

When God sent the Flood, He "sealed" or set apart Noah and his family to be saved. In Egypt, He sealed the firstborn of all the faithful Jewish families by having them apply the blood of a sacrificial lamb to the doorposts of their homes. When He destroyed Jericho, Rahab and her household were set apart to be saved by a scarlet cord. In Elijah's day, He preserved seven thousand people who didn't bow to Baal.

The 144,000 will receive a seal on their foreheads, a seal that is not only internal and spiritual, but also external and visible. It was common in biblical times for masters to brand their slaves on the forehead or the hand to declare ownership. This mark granted them protection from those who might attempt to steal, abuse, or misuse them. In future days—when the seal of the Antichrist signifies death or life (Revelation 13)—the seal of the Father shields His witnesses (14:1). They have been set apart by God for an important task: to preach the gospel in such a way that multitudes will believe.

So in the midst of unparalleled destruction, God extends grace and mercy to a remnant of His people once again so that faith may be preserved, His Word fulfilled, and His kingdom established on the earth.

Blessed Savior, thank You for keeping Your promises, proving Your faithfulness from generation to generation. Thank You for calling me as one of Your own, choosing me to be a part of Your family. As the days grow darker, help me to be a faithful witness to Your great mercy and grace.

Read Revelation 7:1–8 in *The Jeremiah Study Bible.*

REVELATION 7:9–10

After this I looked, and there before me was a great multitude that no one could count, from every nation, tribe, people and language, standing before the throne and before the Lamb. They were wearing white robes and were holding palm branches in their hands. And they cried out in a loud voice:

"Salvation belongs to our God,
who sits on the throne,
and to the Lamb."

21

HOW CAN ANYONE BE SAVED?

(Revelation 7:9–10)

Revelation tells us that during the horrors of the Tribulation, people will cry out to God for deliverance—some of them genuinely. And they will be saved. But how is this possible? How can they hear the gospel and put their trust in Jesus if all the believers have already been taken into heaven in the Rapture?

One way is through the two witnesses God says He will send to preach to them. "I will appoint my two witnesses, and they will prophesy for 1,260 days, clothed in sackcloth" (11:3). These two witnesses will prophesy and do miracles that attest to God and His Word.

There will also be 144,000 born-again Israelites—Jewish believers—who have come to faith in Christ and are sealed (set apart) for God's service during the Tribulation (7:4).

It's possible that God will use all kinds of other ways to bring people to salvation. For instance, there will be millions of Bibles, tracts, and Christian books, as well as Christian videos, websites, articles, and social media posts that will be left behind after Christians are taken to heaven in the Rapture. And the regenerating ministry of the Holy Spirit will not be removed at the Rapture. His restraining of sin will be finished. But when a sinner calls out for salvation, even during the Tribulation, God will hear and save them.

As Tribulation believers read their Bibles, they will share what they have discovered with others. They will begin to prophesy about God's judgment on this sinful world and the more severe judgments that are yet to come. They will preach repentance, which will not make them popular; in fact, it will often lead to their deaths. But as a result, other lives will be saved for eternity.

I must give a strong warning, though. Believe it or not, many people have told me that they think the message of the gospel is "probably" true, but they don't want to be responsible for responding to it just yet: "I'll have my fling now. When the Tribulation starts, then I'll get saved by the first Jewish evangelist I hear."

What a foolish idea!

No one in their right mind would want to be alive on this earth only to experience the excruciating suffering, trial, and torment of the Tribulation. And Scripture explains that during these devastating years, many people will fall under the spell of Satan's lies and be held captive by the great delusion of the Antichrist (2 Thessalonians 2:9–12). They will harden their hearts and refuse to repent, choosing to put their faith in this false savior rather than the Lord Jesus Christ.

So the Bible tells us, "Now is the time of God's favor, now is the day of salvation" (2 Corinthians 6:2).

Lord, help me to lay aside anything in my life that stands between us, anything that would tempt me to turn back from following You. Save me, Jesus! I offer You my whole heart, my whole life, today.

Read Revelation 7:9–10 in *The Jeremiah Study Bible*.

REVELATION 7:13–14

Then one of the elders asked me, "These in white robes—who are they, and where did they come from?"

I answered, "Sir, you know."

And he said, "These are they who have come out of the great tribulation; they have washed their robes and made them white in the blood of the Lamb.

22

SAFELY HOME
(Revelation 7:11–17)

Heaven is full of rejoicing! When the Tribulation is over, John sees a multitude standing before the throne of God. These are all the people who have come to faith in Christ during the Tribulation. They're carrying palm branches and wearing robes that have been made white by the blood of the Lamb. Their trials and troubles are finally over. They are home at last!

Two references in this passage emphasize that these new believers are safe and secure: the palm branches and the promise of God's presence. Palm branches often appear in Scripture as symbols of victory or triumph and the joy and celebration that result. These Tribulation saints triumphed over the enemy through the word of their testimony and the blood of the Lamb, and now they have the additional assurance that God dwells in their midst.

"He who sits on the throne will shelter them with his presence" (7:15).

The verse could also be translated this way: "He who sits on the throne shall spread His tent over them." The Greek word for "tent" is the same one used in John

1:14, which says, "The Word became flesh and made his dwelling [spread His tent] among us." The "tent" is an invitation to dwell together, to be protected and made secure by being brought into the shelter of God's dwelling place.

As the psalmist exclaimed, "How lovely is your dwelling place, LORD Almighty! My soul yearns, even faints, for the courts of the LORD; my heart and my flesh cry out for the living God" (Psalm 84:1–2).

The multitude now standing before God's throne cries out in worship: "Salvation belongs to our God, who sits on the throne, and to the Lamb" (Revelation 7:10).

The angels say, "Amen!" and then add their own anthem of praise.

Revelation 7:17 reminds us that Jesus is both the Lamb of God and the Good Shepherd. As the Lamb, He was slain before the foundation of the world to purchase our salvation. As the Shepherd, He has made us the sheep of His pasture. He watches over us and tenderly cares for us as His own.

The new believers have suffered greatly at the hands of the Antichrist. On earth, they lost everything. They experienced hunger and starvation, because without the mark of the beast, they were unable to buy food (13:17). They were without shelter, without protection. They were hunted and killed. But now everything that they lacked during the Tribulation is given to them by their Shepherd in heaven, and it cannot be taken from them. The Shepherd promises that "never again will they hunger; never again will they thirst" (7:16).

Here they will experience complete healing and restoration. Here they will find rest, and God "will wipe every tear from their eyes" (21:4).

God of all comfort, comfort me with Your presence today. Be with all those who suffer, all those who are afflicted. How we long for the day when we see You face-to-face and know that our journey is complete, that we are safely home!

Read Revelation 7:11–17 in *The Jeremiah Study Bible.*

REVELATION 8:1–3, 5

When he opened the seventh seal, there was silence in heaven for about half an hour.

And I saw the seven angels who stand before God, and seven trumpets were given to them.

Another angel, who had a golden censer, came and stood at the altar. . . . Then the angel took the censer, filled it with fire from the altar, and hurled it on the earth; and there came peals of thunder, rumblings, flashes of lightning and an earthquake.

23

A MOMENT OF SILENCE

(Revelation 8:1–5)

The silence is deafening. Up until now, Revelation tells us, the heavens have been filled with the sounds of worship. Choirs of angels and saints from every age have exulted in singing God's praises. Believers have been bowing before His throne at regular intervals, casting their crowns at His feet, honoring Him with everything they are and everything they have.

But what is about to take place is so solemn, so serious, that all the activity around the throne of God—all the expressions of praise and adoration—suddenly cease.

When the seventh seal is opened, seven trumpet judgments are released. The world, which has been ruined by humans under the judgment of the first six seals (6:1–17), is about to become a world ruled by Satan under the judgment of the trumpet (8:6). The entire planet will be handed over to the beast. The devil's false messiah—the Antichrist, the man of sin—begins to take control. But even this is done under the sovereignty of God.

"See, it is I who created the blacksmith who fans the coals into flame and forges a weapon fit for its work. And it is I who have created the destroyer to wreak havoc." (Isaiah 54:16)

Everything is unfolding according to God's plan.

An angel steps forward with a golden censer and offers the prayers of the saints on the altar before the throne of God. I believe these are the prayers of the Tribulation martyrs in Revelation 6:9–10. They have asked God to take action, to avenge them, and to judge swiftly those responsible for their suffering and deaths.

How long will the enemy mock you, God? Will the foe revile your name forever? . . . How long, LORD, will the wicked, how long will the wicked be jubilant? . . . How long must your servant wait? When will you punish my persecutors? (Psalm 74:10, 94:3, 119:84)

As soon as their pleas for God's vindication ascend, God's judgment descends; their prayers are answered.

The angel fills the golden censer with fire from the altar and throws it on the earth, and "there came peals of thunder, rumblings, flashes of lightning and an earthquake" (Revelation 8:5).

Seven angels now stand ready to sound seven trumpets, pouring out God's righteous wrath.

In the Old Testament, trumpets summoned people to worship and prepared people for war (Numbers 10). The seven trumpets here signal God's final intervention, His last judgment on the earth, before Christ comes to establish His eternal kingdom.

But who can endure the day of his coming? Who can stand when he appears? (Malachi 3:2)

Holy God, You are just and righteous in all Your ways; Your judgments are true and right. If You, Lord, kept a record of sins, who could stand? I'm forever grateful that with You there is forgiveness, so that we might learn to fear You—to humbly serve You with awe and reverence. I bow before You and offer You my silence as I meditate on Your Word to me today.

Read Revelation 8:1–5 in *The Jeremiah Study Bible*.

REVELATION 8:7–10, 12

The first angel sounded his trumpet, and there came hail and fire mixed with blood, and it was hurled down on the earth. A third of the earth was burned up, a third of the trees were burned up, and all the green grass was burned up.

The second angel sounded his trumpet, and something like a huge mountain, all ablaze, was thrown into the sea. A third of the sea turned into blood, a third of the living creatures in the sea died, and a third of the ships were destroyed.

The third angel sounded his trumpet, and a great star, blazing like a torch, fell from the sky on a third of the rivers and on the springs of water— . . .

The fourth angel sounded his trumpet, and a third of the sun was struck, a third of the moon, and a third of the stars, so that a third of them turned dark. A third of the day was without light, and also a third of the night.

24

WHEN ALL HELL BREAKS LOOSE

(Revelation 8:6–13)

The time has come. In Revelation 5, a scroll was presented to the Lamb that was slain—the only one found worthy to open it. It has been gradually unsealed and unrolled, one form of judgment coming after another, until the earth will finally be delivered into the hands of the King of kings, its rightful owner. The seventh seal on the scroll unleashes the seven trumpet judgments—the final judgment—of God upon the earth.

At the sound of the first trumpet, the earth suffers terrible ecological devastation. An angel hurls down "hail and fire mixed with blood," and a third of all vegetation is destroyed (8:7).

With the second trumpet, "something like a huge mountain, all ablaze, was thrown into the sea" (8:8). As a result, a third of the seas turn to blood and a third of the ships are destroyed.

The third trumpet causes a "great star" called "Wormwood" to fall from heaven and poison one-third of the freshwater rivers and springs (8:10–11). Wormwood is a plant with a bitter taste that symbolizes the bitterness of sorrow and calamity (Jeremiah 9:15). It's hard to imagine the resulting chaos on earth when a third of the world's population has no clean water to drink. Many people will die as a result of their contaminated water supply.

When the fourth trumpet sounds, one-third of the heavens go dark, causing drastic atmospheric changes, including an extreme decrease in temperature. A third of these heavenly bodies will suddenly change their normal functions and positions, including their orbits. Remember, Jesus told us that we would know we were living in the last days by the signs in the sun, moon, and stars (Luke 21:25).

Suddenly John sees an eagle "flying in midair" (8:13). It warns the inhabitants of the earth that the remaining three trumpets will usher in an era of even greater judgment. Gradually, the earth is being handed over to Satan for the destruction he will wreak through his agent, the Antichrist.

Consider what it will be like to be on earth when the events in Revelation 8 take place. You lose friends, coworkers, and neighbors in large numbers. You try to contact loved ones, but all communication systems have been damaged. The news media is filled with reports of chaos, destruction, and death. And then you begin to hear of a leader who claims to be able to bring peace, restore law and order, stabilize the government and the economy, and provide the world's citizens with all they need to survive. Nearly everyone in the world, with the exception of those who retain some spiritual discernment, will eagerly follow his leadership.

Of course this leader is really "the man of lawlessness" (2 Thessalonians 2:3), and his ultimate goal is world domination—to command the obedience and worship of all mankind.

Lord, keep me from the deceit of the enemy today. Make me alert and watchful as I look for Your appearing. How I long for the day when You reclaim Your world and establish Your eternal kingdom! Until then, help me to serve You faithfully and share Your gospel boldly, so that others, too, will be safe in heaven when the trumpet judgments unfold on earth.

Read Revelation 8:6–13 in *The Jeremiah Study Bible.*

REVELATION 9:1–3, 6

The fifth angel sounded his trumpet, and I saw a star that had fallen from the sky to the earth. The star was given the key to the shaft of the Abyss. When he opened the Abyss, smoke rose from it like the smoke from a gigantic furnace. The sun and sky were darkened by the smoke from the Abyss. And out of the smoke locusts came down on the earth and were given power like that of scorpions of the earth. . . . During those days people will seek death but will not find it; they will long to die, but death will elude them.

25

HELL IS FOR REAL

(Revelation 9:1–12)

Regardless of what some people think, hell is not a state of mind, a myth, or a mild curse word. According to the Bible, it's a literal place filled with horrors, a great pit of fire and smoke, populated by terrifying creatures that inflict pain and suffering. The Tribulation is only a preview of coming destruction.

In Revelation 9, the "star" or supernatural being that falls to earth is Satan. As part of His judgment on a sinful world, God allows Satan to open the doors to the "Abyss" and unleash extraordinary demonic power to wreak havoc on the earth (9:2).

The Abyss is mentioned in several other places in Scripture. In Luke 8, when Jesus encountered demons in a man, the demons begged Him not to send them to the Abyss (Luke 8:31). In Jude 6, we learn that the angels confined in the Abyss are "bound with everlasting chains for judgment on the great Day." These angels (now called demons) participated in a rebellion against God and have been assigned to the Abyss until they will be judged and cast into the "eternal fire" (Matthew 25:41).

When Satan opens the Abyss, the sky is darkened by the smoke that pours forth from it. We know that the "locusts" that come down from the smoke are not real locusts because they do not harm the vegetation (Revelation 9:4), they have a king (9:11), and God promised never to release locusts in judgment again (Exodus 10:14). Rather, "locusts" is a metaphor for a gigantic swarm of demons spreading over the earth. These locusts immediately set out to attack those who are not "sealed" or set apart by God.

What will be the result of thousands of demons set loose throughout the earth during the Tribulation? It will be a horrific experience for those who are left to endure it. The torment these demons inflict will be both painful and protracted—like the sting of a scorpion—yet it will not lead to death (Revelation 9:5). Many people on earth at that time will long for death as an escape from the excruciating pain but they will be unable to die.

If this seems unfair or unjust for a loving God to allow, remember that, in the words of the hymn by Fanny Crosby, "The vilest offender who truly believes / That moment from Jesus a pardon receives."

Those who seek His mercy find it.

Those who reject it and reject Him—those who have delighted in their wickedness, those who have flaunted their sin, those who have tormented and victimized others without shame or remorse—well, they've been warned. And they have made their choice.

Those who are in the Lord's will have His name on their foreheads and will be protected from the demonic attack (22:4). They will continue to experience His peace, His provision, and His protection. He will be their refuge, their shelter in the time of storm (Psalm 61:4).

Lord God, when I think of the horrors of hell, I'm so grateful that I belong to You! Thank You for setting Your seal upon me and claiming me as Your own. Help me to live a life worthy of Your calling, for Your honor and glory.

Read Revelation 9:1–12 in *The Jeremiah Study Bible.*

REVELATION 9:13–15, 20

The sixth angel sounded his trumpet, and I heard a voice coming from the four horns of the golden altar that is before God. It said to the sixth angel who had the trumpet, "Release the four angels who are bound at the great river Euphrates." And the four angels who had been kept ready for this very hour and day and month and year were released to kill a third of mankind. . . .

The rest of mankind who were not killed by these plagues still did not repent of the work of their hands; they did not stop worshiping demons, and idols of gold, silver, bronze, stone and wood—idols that cannot see or hear or walk.

26

NO TURNING BACK
(Revelation 9:13–21)

One of the most sobering revelations in the book of Revelation is that some people are literally hell-bent on their own destruction. Nothing and no one can turn them back from the dark path they have chosen. Even in the face of the most extraordinary crisis or tragedy, they will not humble themselves and cry out to God for help.

Revelation 6:8 began with 25 percent of the world's population being killed by famine, plagues, and wild beasts. Now, with the sounding of the sixth trumpet, one-third of the remaining 75 percent will be killed in battle. So with the completion of this judgment, nearly half the world's population will have been wiped from the face of the earth. Revelation 9:16 says that this will be accomplished by an army of two hundred million people. This number is almost twice as many troops as the combined Allied and Axis powers when they were at peak strengths during World War II!

Revelation 16:12 describes the sixth bowl judgment, which dries out the Euphrates River. Most commentators believe that this makes it possible for this army to be led by "kings from the East" (16:12) to march westward, toward and against Israel.

John's description of the troops—the horses and their riders—is both fantastic and terrifying: fiery breastplates, horses' heads like lions, fire, smoke, and brimstone. Some scholars believe he's describing, from his first-century perspective, implements of modern warfare, such as we see on the world's battlefields today. Whatever the exact manifestation of that war, we know that the largest army in the history of the world will cross the dry riverbed of the Euphrates and cause epic destruction.

What's even more grim than the description of this destruction is the depiction of mankind's response. The people do not repent. They do not beg God for forgiveness or mercy. They do not ask Him to rescue or deliver them (9:20–21). Like Pharaoh in the days of Moses, they harden their hearts and continue engaging in evil.

> For this people's heart has become calloused;
>> they hardly hear with their ears,
>> and they have closed their eyes.
> Otherwise they might see with their eyes,
>> hear with their ears,
>> understand with their hearts
> and turn, and I would heal them. (Acts 28:27)

Fear of pain or painful consequences can sometimes motivate people to temporarily modify their behavior. But true repentance and lasting change—heart change—can only take place in response to the gospel.

The devastation we witness as we read Revelation is a powerful reminder to hold fast to the Truth we have received.

Don't let your heart be hardened by sin's deceitfulness today. "Repent, then, and turn to God, so that your sins may be wiped out, that times of refreshing may come from the Lord" (Acts 3:19).

Lord Jesus, I humbly ask for Your forgiveness, mercy, and grace. Create in me a clean heart. Keep it tender and responsive to Your Word. Show me my disobedient and offensive actions and lead me in the way everlasting.

Read Revelation 9:13–21 in *The Jeremiah Study Bible*.

REVELATION 10:1–4

Then I saw another mighty angel coming down from heaven. He was robed in a cloud, with a rainbow above his head; his face was like the sun, and his legs were like fiery pillars. He was holding a little scroll, which lay open in his hand. He planted his right foot on the sea and his left foot on the land, and he gave a loud shout like the roar of a lion. When he shouted, the voices of the seven thunders spoke. And when the seven thunders spoke, I was about to write; but I heard a voice from heaven say, "Seal up what the seven thunders have said and do not write it down."

27

COULD YOU USE
SOME GOOD NEWS?
(Revelation 10:1–11)

The book of Revelation describes dark days to come, so dark it can feel overwhelming. But in the midst of this darkness, we find several interludes of grace—passages that provide relief and hope for every believer. In Revelation 10, we're offered glimpses of God's steadfast love. We find encouragement in the assurance that however depressing the events of the end times might seem, He is still on His throne. The world is not without His witness, and even in judgment, there is mercy.

In John's vision in Revelation 10:1, an angel brings a message of hope to the earth. This angel has appeared twice before. First, he came as the prophet, holding back judgments in order that the 144,000 could be sealed (7:2). Then, he came as the priest, presenting the prayers of the saints to God (8:4). Here, he comes as the king, claiming his dominion.

I believe this is the Angel of Jehovah, the Lord Himself. This mighty angel is clothed with a cloud, which symbolizes the presence of God (Exodus 16:10). The angel is also crowned with a rainbow, which reminds us of the rainbow around God's throne (Revelation 4:3). The angel is covered in glory, which fits the shining face of Jesus Christ (1:16). And His feet, like "fiery pillars" (10:1), are similar to the feet of Christ in Revelation 1:15, which were "like bronze glowing in a furnace."

The Angel of Jehovah has come to take possession of heaven and earth. His triumphant stance is a picture of His sovereignty, and the open scroll is a sign of His right to possess the earth. The message He brings is one of reassurance and comfort: He is in control.

When the Angel of Jehovah makes His announcement, He speaks with "a loud shout like the roar of a lion" (10:3). Seven thunders reverberate across the earth.

> God's voice thunders in marvelous ways;
>> he does great things beyond our
>>> understanding. (Job 37:5)

What did the angel tell John in the seven thunders? We don't know. For the first and only time in this book, John is forbidden to reveal the content of the revelation he receives—a reminder that "the secret things belong to the LORD our God" (Deuteronomy 29:29).

What mystery will be accomplished—and revealed—when the judgments are complete? I believe it is the answer to why Satan has been allowed to work his evil for thousands of years and what God has planned for

His ultimate triumph, when He banishes Satan and evil once and for all and fulfills His glorious purpose for the ages.

This message is good news! When we look around our world and feel hopeless, when it seems evil has the upper hand, we need to remember that our eternal, omnipotent, just, and merciful God is still on His throne.

Like those who suffer in the Tribulation, we can take courage in the knowledge that our times are in His hands. Everything is unfolding according to His sovereign plan. And He *will* reign forever and ever. Hallelujah!

Lord, whenever I'm tempted to believe that evil will triumph, remind me to take comfort in the truth of Your Word. Jesus, You are—and will always be—victorious, now and forever!

Read Revelation 10:1–11 in *The Jeremiah Study Bible.*

REVELATION 11:1, 3

I was given a reed like a measuring rod and was told, "Go and measure the temple of God and the altar, with its worshipers. . . . And I will appoint my two witnesses, and they will prophesy for 1,260 days, clothed in sackcloth."

28

WITHOUT EXCUSE
(Revelation 11:1–6)

J erusalem is the most embattled city in history, but her most dramatic days are yet to come. Revelation 11 reveals that one day Jerusalem will be called to account for her sinful ways. And the entire world will watch what happens next!

Sometime during the Tribulation, the temple will be rebuilt by the Jewish people, and the Antichrist will set himself up to take the place of God in Jewish worship (2 Thessalonians 2:4). The Antichrist will make a covenant with Israel, but three and a half years later, he'll break that covenant and defile the temple.

In Revelation 11:1, John is told to act out the prophecy. "I was given a reed like a measuring rod and was told, 'Go and measure the temple of God and the altar, with its worshipers.'" In Scripture, a rod indicates judgment. John is measuring God's people, the Jews, and those who choose to worship the Antichrist will be judged. They'll experience storms and plagues and drought. There will be plenty of suffering to go around.

Yet in the midst of these devastating circumstances, God will send two men to begin witnessing to His people. They will preach the gospel with power throughout the Jewish world.

Many scholars find this chapter of Revelation difficult to interpret, but it helps to understand that these two witnesses are real human beings, not symbols. It's likely that the two witnesses are Moses and Elijah, representing the Law and the Prophets. They wear sackcloth because they are mourning the spiritual condition of Israel. In images drawn from the Old Testament, they are called olive trees and lampstands to signify their ministry of life and light in darkness, through the power of the Holy Spirit (Zechariah 4:2–4, 11–12).

The two witnesses will expose sin and hypocrisy, call the people to repentance, and warn them of future judgments, even worse than those they have already endured. And until the two men finish denouncing wickedness and proclaiming Christ, they will be supernaturally protected. These two witnesses will be given the power not only to preach but also to inflict judgment on those who try to harm them (Revelation 11:5). They will boldly preach against the Antichrist who blasphemes God (Revelation 13).

Believe it or not, we can find great comfort in this challenging chapter of Scripture. The two witnesses are evidence that God is truly merciful and just. He has given the world (and will keep giving the world) every chance for redemption.

In the end times, those who finally reject Him will do so willfully, knowingly, and freely. It's not as if they've never heard the gospel, never seen a display of God's miraculous power, never had the opportunity to repent and receive His salvation.

They simply don't want it.

Our job as His witnesses today is not to try to make people *want* to be saved but to shine His light and share our faith with those who *do*.

Lord Jesus, today I pray for the peace of the troubled city of Jerusalem. I pray that the people living there will find peace in You. Help me to be a bold and fearless witness to those around me who are hungry and searching for You.

Read Revelation 11:1–6 in *The Jeremiah Study Bible.*

REVELATION 11:7–8, 11–12

Now when they have finished their testimony, the beast that comes up from the Abyss will attack them, and overpower and kill them. Their bodies will lie in the public square of the great city— which is figuratively called Sodom and Egypt— where also their Lord was crucified. . . .

But after the three and a half days the breath of life from God entered them, and they stood on their feet, and terror struck those who saw them. Then they heard a loud voice from heaven saying to them, "Come up here." And they went up to heaven in a cloud, while their enemies looked on.

29

WITHOUT HONOR

(Revelation 11:7–14)

The Scripture tells us that the two witnesses (or prophets) who appear during the Tribulation arouse intense interest and, among some people, completely opposite responses. Some who hear the witnesses preaching fall on their knees and repent, but many others will react in an irrational, emotional, and violent frenzy.

The new ruler, "the beast that comes up from the Abyss" (11:7), otherwise known as the Antichrist, orders the two men to be publicly executed. Killing these two witnesses is, in fact, the first official act he uses to establish widespread support among his following. The witnesses' deaths are turned into an occasion for worldwide celebration, most especially in Jerusalem—the center of the Antichrist's activity. The wicked give each other gifts, rejoicing in the demise of these tormented preachers.

For three and a half days, the witnesses' dead bodies are displayed in Jerusalem. The length of time indicates that they are genuinely and indisputably dead. Everyone can see that it is so.

Revelation 11:9 tells us that some "from every people, tribe, language and nation will gaze on their bodies and refuse them burial." Jewish law requires burial immediately upon death, even for a criminal (Deuteronomy 21:22–23). With this act, the people attempt to express contempt and to expose the witnesses' shame and dishonor—but all this does is reveal, instead, they are the ones without a shred of decency or honor.

Suddenly, in the midst of the jubilation, the laughter dies. The cheers end abruptly. The crowd stands frozen in fear, as a thundering voice from heaven calls to the two witnesses: "Come up here" (Revelation 11:12).

Jesus once told His disciples, "Don't be afraid. . . . Whoever acknowledges me before others, I will also acknowledge before my Father in heaven" (Matthew 10:31–32).

Now, before the eyes of all the world, God honors those who have honored Him. He supernaturally resurrects His two witnesses and restores them to life. They rise to heaven in a cloud, while their enemies look on, aghast (Revelation 11:12).

The witnesses' ascension fills the world with fear and dread. The Antichrist attempts to explain the rapture of the prisoners, but this is one miracle he will not be able to counterfeit or replicate.

Next, immediately after the two witnesses are raptured, the city of Jerusalem is shaken by a tremendous earthquake. It destroys one-tenth of the city and claims the lives of seven thousand corrupt city leaders.

Unbelievably, those who are left alive cry out to God in terror—but not in repentance! Their hearts are pounding in fear, not breaking under conviction. Their response is ultimately temporary and insincere.

My prayer is that we will all be like the two witnesses, that we will honor Him with more than our lips and that we will remain faithful until the end, unlike those who call on God out of fear one minute and forget Him the next.

Lord, keep my heart open and my conscience tender toward You. Help me today to remain faithful to Your Word, even in times of intense trial or testing. Show me how to boldly proclaim Your gospel to everyone who has ears to hear.

Read Revelation 11:7–14 in *The Jeremiah Study Bible.*

REVELATION 11:15–17

The seventh angel sounded his trumpet, and there were loud voices in heaven, which said:

"The kingdom of the world has become

the kingdom of our Lord and of his Messiah,

and he will reign for ever and ever."

And the twenty-four elders, who were seated on their thrones before God, fell on their faces and worshiped God, saying:

"We give thanks to you, Lord God Almighty,

the One who is and who was,

because you have taken your great power

and have begun to reign."

30

CORONATION DAY

The book of Revelation is so dismal from chapters 5 to 11 that, without the little interludes where we're allowed a glimpse of heaven, we might lose heart. Here in Revelation 11, we receive a sneak preview, from a heavenly perspective, of the coronation of Christ. It depicts the transition of power to the King of kings and Lord of lords. What a day that will be!

Some believers are surprised to discover that the "kingdom" and "kingdom of the world" (11:15) do not already belong to Christ. Rather, they are temporarily under Satan's authority (Matthew 12:26; 2 Corinthians 4:4; Ephesians 2:2). Of course, God obviously has ultimate authority over the world and all that happens in it, but He has allowed Satan to have dominion at present.

But not for long!

The voices in heaven proclaim that the kingdoms of the world have become "the kingdom of our Lord and of his Messiah" (Revelation 11:15).

Reflecting on this truth, hymnwriter Matthew Bridges exclaimed:

Crown him with many crowns,
the Lamb upon his throne.
Hark! how the heavenly anthem drowns
all music but its own.
Awake, my soul, and sing
of him who died for thee,
and hail him as thy matchless king
through all eternity.

When the seventh trumpet sounds, the twenty-four elders fall down and worship God. They rejoice to see their King begin His triumphant and eternal reign. The grand celebration takes place after God has defeated His enemies at the Battle of Armageddon.

This is the day Paul looked forward to in Philippians 2:7–11, when he said of Jesus:

Rather, he made himself nothing
by taking the very nature of a servant,
being made in human likeness.
And being found in appearance as a man,
he humbled himself
by becoming obedient to death—
even death on a cross!
Therefore God exalted him to the highest place
and gave him the name that is above every name,
that at the name of Jesus every knee should bow,

in heaven and on earth and under the earth,
and every tongue acknowledge that Jesus Christ
is Lord,
to the glory of God the Father.

There have been times in the history of the world that have been considered "golden ages," but we have never seen anything yet like the unity, the beauty, the peace, and the prosperity that God has in store for all of us when He establishes His eternal kingdom. We can only try to imagine . . .

Lord Jesus, You are worthy to receive all my worship! I praise Your glorious name! And I give thanks for all You have done for me. I eagerly anticipate celebrating Your coronation day and Your eternal reign.

Read Revelation 11:15–17 in *The Jeremiah Study Bible.*

REVELATION 11:18

The nations were angry,
and your wrath has come.
The time has come for judging the dead,
and for rewarding your servants the
prophets
and your people who revere your name,
both great and small—
and for destroying those who destroy the
earth."

31

SPOILER ALERT
(Revelation 11:18–19)

Have you ever watched a movie or read a book full of thrilling twists and turns turns and suddenly found yourself at a loss to follow the plot? You may not be a fan of online reviews that warn: "Spoiler Alert" but sometimes you need a few helpful clues!

Revelation 11:18 is a bit like a review with spoilers. It contains a "prophetic snapshot"—an overview of what will happen in the rest of Revelation. But we are not given everything at once. There are large gaps of time between the outpourings of God's wrath, the judgment of the dead, the reward of the faithful, and the destruction of those who destroy the earth.

As we review the highlights of the plot still unfolding, it's helpful to remember that the events described here are separated by more than a thousand years, though they appear to happen one right after another. This is heaven's perspective, one vast picture.

Here are the key points:

1. *The nations are angry.* Earlier we saw how the leaders of Jerusalem killed God's witnesses. By the end of the Tribulation, the kingdoms of this

world will unite against God Himself, and He will pour out His wrath on those who oppose Him (Psalm 2:1–5).

2. *God judges the dead.* At the Great White Throne Judgment, all the unsaved from every age in history are called to appear before the Righteous Judge (Revelation 20:13). Believers, on the other hand, will be brought before the Judgment Seat of Christ (2 Corinthians 5:10), not to determine their salvation, but to judge their works for Christ.

3. *Rewards are given to believers.* The believers of the Old Testament—and those who became believers during the Tribulation—now receive their rewards. Church-age believers have already received their rewards at the Judgment Seat of Christ, after the Rapture.

4. *God destroys those who destroyed the earth.* The demons who have been turned loose to wreak havoc during the Tribulation will, in turn, be destroyed by our sovereign Lord.

Revelation 11:18–19 shows us that everything that needs to happen to establish God's kingdom will happen—just as He promised.

It also gives us yet another picture of God's amazing love, mercy, and grace. Amidst the cataclysmic events of the Tribulation, we look into the heavenly temple and see the ark of the covenant—the precious symbol of the presence and power of God in the midst of the Jewish people (11:19). This vision of the ark being returned to the temple in heaven would have greatly encouraged the suffering people to whom John originally sent this revelation.

Verse 19 reminds us that God is present even in the most difficult times in our lives. He's still there during the Tribulation for all who come to Him in those terrifying days. Those who have genuine faith will hear His Truth, see His provision, and experience His life-giving, life-changing power.

As we glimpse into the dark days ahead, God's faithfulness to His covenant provides an anchor for the soul. It's a comfort for all who—even now—face overwhelming circumstances (Hebrews 6:19).

God, whatever circumstances I face today, help me hold fast to Your covenant promises of salvation, provision, and peace. Your faithfulness to Your Word is the anchor of my soul, keeping me steady through the storms.

Read Revelation 11:18–19 in *The Jeremiah Study Bible.*

REVELATION 12:1–4

A great sign appeared in heaven: a woman clothed with the sun, with the moon under her feet and a crown of twelve stars on her head. She was pregnant and cried out in pain as she was about to give birth. Then another sign appeared in heaven: an enormous red dragon with seven heads and ten horns and seven crowns on its heads. Its tail swept a third of the stars out of the sky and flung them to the earth. The dragon stood in front of the woman who was about to give birth, so that it might devour her child the moment he was born.

32

THE BATTLE UNSEEN

(Revelation 12:1–4)

The Bible tells us that although we can't see it, a great war is being waged in the heavens. This war has a direct impact on our lives and on events that take place here on earth.

> For our struggle is not against flesh and blood, but against the rulers, against the authorities, against the powers of this dark world and against the spiritual forces of evil in the heavenly realms. (Ephesians 6:12)

In Revelation 12, we get a behind-the-scenes look at this warfare—a glimpse from heaven's perspective. The key combatants are God and Satan, along with their heavenly armies (angels) and the humans who carry out the conflict being waged in the supernatural realm here on earth.

First, we're introduced to a woman who represents Israel, described by Old Testament prophets as a woman in labor (Micah 4:9–10). In Revelation 12, she gives birth to a child—the Lord Jesus Christ. Paul pointed out in Romans 9:5 that Christ came from the Jewish nation. This woman, Israel, is the one whom "an enormous red dragon"—Satan—seeks to destroy (Revelation 12:3).

Inspired by this description of a dragon, modern caricatures of the devil sometimes portray him with horns and a tail. But Revelation 12:3 isn't meant to be a literal description of his physical appearance. The term *dragon* is a symbolic reference to his vile, cruel, and calculating nature. The color red represents war, bloodshed, and death—which follow him everywhere he goes. The seven heads convey his authority and his worldwide power.

We're told here in Revelation 12:4 that Satan had once "swept a third of the stars out of the sky and flung them to the earth." This refers to the epic event that happened ages ago, when Satan was expelled from heaven because of his rebellion against God (Isaiah 14). When he fell, one-third of the angels (his followers) fell with him and were thrown to the earth. (Elsewhere in Scripture angels are called stars; see Isaiah 14:12 and Job 38:7.) Some of these fallen angels are already confined to the Abyss, but many are active as Satan's servants in our world.

In this scene, the dragon stands ready to devour the Child who is about to be born. We see that Satan's purpose has always been to destroy Christ (Matthew 2:16), to keep Him from fulfilling the promise God made to

Eve in the Garden of Eden, that her seed would one day crush the head of the serpent (Genesis 3:15).

As apologist C. S. Lewis once observed, "There is no neutral ground in the universe. Every square inch, every split second is claimed by God and counterclaimed by Satan."

And we are not helpless bystanders or hapless casualties in this war. We're active participants, for one side or the other.

> Therefore put on the full armor of God, so that when the day of evil comes, you may be able to stand your ground. (Ephesians 6:13)

Lord Jesus, I realize that Your enemy and mine, the devil, prowls around like a roaring lion looking for someone to devour. Help me to be alert and of sober mind. Give me the courage and strength to take a stand for Your kingdom and Your glory.

Read Revelation 12:1–4 in *The Jeremiah Study Bible*.

REVELATION 12:5, 9

She gave birth to a son, a male child, who "will rule all the nations with an iron scepter." And her child was snatched up to God and to his throne. . . .

The great dragon was hurled down—that ancient serpent called the devil, or Satan, who leads the whole world astray. He was hurled to the earth, and his angels with him.

33

ALL IN GOD'S TIME
(Revelation 12:5–9)

W e've learned that Satan was cast out of heaven
because he sought to receive the worship that
belongs to God alone, and that the war between God
and Satan and their angels has been going on ever since.

Revelation 12:5 gives us a summary, again from
heaven's perspective, of three of the most significant
events in the life of Christ. First, we see His incarnation—when the "woman" (Israel) "gave birth to a son,
a male child" (Isaiah 7:14); next, His ascension—
"her child was snatched up to God and to his throne"
(Revelation 12:5); and finally, His Second Coming—
when He will rule all the nations with an iron scepter
(Revelation 2:27).

Some may wonder, *If Satan was defeated at the cross
of Christ, then why does he seem to be winning?*

Why does it appear that Satan is gaining ground
on earth today? And most importantly, why is God
waiting until the end of history to destroy Satan? Why
doesn't God destroy him now?

Perhaps the best way to reconcile what seems to
be a disconnect between Satan's ultimate fate and his

present freedom is to understand that the cross was (in essence) a legal transaction. Christ's sacrifice at Calvary appeased the wrath of God. He paid the penalty for our sin once and for all. So through His death and resurrection, He legally defeated and disarmed Satan.

But as with most legal judgments, there is a time lapse between legislation and enforcement. The victory that was won at the cross will take full effect at the end of the Millennium. In the meantime, the Church stands against Satan and declares victory on the legal grounds we have in the death and resurrection of Jesus Christ.

We may not fully understand God's timing, at least not on this side of heaven, or why He has chosen to allow things to unfold the way He has. But as Jesus explained in Matthew 5:18:

> Truly I tell you, until heaven and earth disappear, not the smallest letter, not the least stroke of a pen, will by any means disappear from the Law until everything is accomplished.

For whatever reason there are prophecies in Scripture yet to be fulfilled and necessary—even crucial—events that must take place. Most importantly, there are still souls who have yet to enter into Christ's kingdom.

> The Lord is not slow in keeping his promise, as some understand slowness. Instead he is patient

with you, not wanting anyone to perish, but everyone to come to repentance. (2 Peter 3:9)

He waited for each one of us to come to a saving knowledge of Him. We must be patient and stand strong while we wait for the others—the rest of our sisters and brothers—to find their way to Him.

Lord Jesus, as my eyes are opened to the spiritual warfare raging around me, teach me to persevere in prayer and stand firm in the forgiveness and freedom I've found in You. Let me be a light in the darkness, leading others to trust in You too.

Read Revelation 12:5–9 in *The Jeremiah Study Bible*.

REVELATION 12:10–11

Then I heard a loud voice in heaven say:
  "Now have come the salvation and the power
    and the kingdom of our God,
    and the authority of his Messiah.
  For the accuser of our brothers and sisters,
    who accuses them before our God day
  and night,
    has been hurled down.
  They triumphed over him
    by the blood of the Lamb
    and by the word of their testimony;
  they did not love their lives so much
    as to shrink from death."

34

SILENCING
THE ACCUSER

(Revelation 12:10–12)

Satan is a mystery to many people. As a result, they end up placing themselves at his disposal, not understanding his power *or their power against him*. The Bible reminds us that while Satan appears to have full reign against believers, his power is limited, and he can be overcome. In Revelation, we see Satan's downward spiral—from heaven to earth, then from earth to the Abyss, and finally from the Abyss to the lake of fire.

In order to understand what Revelation says about Satan's fall, it's helpful to look back at the story of Job. There we see that Satan, though expelled from heaven, still has access to God's throne. Satan accused Job of not truly being faithful to God. He asked God's permission to test Job, and God gave it. Yet despite Satan's attacks, Job remained faithful—just as God said he would.

Satan is depicted as the "accuser of our brothers and sisters" (Revelation 12:10). But as Christians, "we have an advocate with the Father—Jesus Christ, the Righteous One" (1 John 2:1), who defends us when the accuser comes to attack us. Revelation 12 describes the last period in Satan's existence, when he has the freedom to enter God's presence. After a war against Michael and his angels, Satan and his evil angels are cast out of heaven to earth, never again to accuse believers before the throne of God (12:10).

When Satan is thrown out of heaven, there is great rejoicing, perhaps led by one of the martyrs described in Revelation 6:9–10. Even in their deaths, the martyrs have overcome Satan in three ways:

1. *By the blood of the Lamb.* "'Come now, let us settle the matter,' says the LORD. 'Though your sins are like scarlet, they shall be as white as snow; though they are red as crimson, they shall be like wool'" (Isaiah 1:18). When Jesus shed His blood at the cross, all our sins were paid for— meaning that Satan has no grounds on which to accuse the repentant, faithful believer.

2. *By the word of their testimony.* Jesus said, "Whoever acknowledges me before others, I will also acknowledge before my Father in heaven" (Matthew 10:32). He claims those who publicly acknowledge Him as members of His kingdom, His family; He asserts that they are under His protection. He will rescue them, deliver them, and avenge them.

3. *By loving God more than life itself.* History is filled with those who "did not love their lives so much as to shrink from death" (Revelation 12:11). Satan cannot overcome these people. They are free to live in complete obedience to the Lord because they know Satan has no power to separate them from the love of Christ (Romans 8:38–39).

This is the same way Christians overcome Satan today. The death and resurrection of Christ is the basis for all victory over Satan. Therefore, believers need not fear the ultimate death—separation from Him ("the second death" [Revelation 2:11; 20:6])—because our salvation is certain.

Jesus, You are victorious over sin, over Satan, over death and hell. Teach me how to follow Your example, to stand firm and overcome the enemy, that I may be found faithful and bring glory and honor to You.

Read Revelation 12:10–12 in *The Jeremiah Study Bible.*

REVELATION 12:13–14

When the dragon saw that he had been hurled to the earth, he pursued the woman who had given birth to the male child. The woman was given the two wings of a great eagle, so that she might fly to the place prepared for her in the wilderness, where she would be taken care of for a time, times and half a time, out of the serpent's reach.

35

FROM A CERTAIN POINT OF VIEW

(Revelation 12:13–17)

It almost sounds like an ancient myth or fairy tale, a long-lost fable of some epic adventure. But the story in Revelation 12 is absolutely true. It's just presented to us from a certain point of view—the view of heaven. It's written in symbol and metaphor, but the reality of it reverberates across the universe.

Satan—the "dragon" or "serpent"—has been ousted from heaven. When he comes to earth, he is in a blazing fury "because he knows that his time is short" (12:12). Soon, he will be bound for a thousand years and then doomed—thrown into the Lake of Fire for all eternity. This explains the intensity of the evil he perpetrates during the Tribulation. It's his last chance to do his very worst.

The dragon (Satan) viciously persecutes a woman (Israel), who has given birth to a male child (Jesus). Satan has been harassing, attacking, and persecuting God's chosen people throughout their existence (Zechariah 3:1). In Revelation 12:17, we learn that the dragon is especially angry with the redeemed Jews—

the 144,000 witnesses who refuse to take the mark of the beast and who "keep God's commands and hold fast their testimony about Jesus."

Now he has one final shot to take. Satan wants to destroy Israel utterly and completely, particularly as the time draws near for the Messiah to return to earth to establish His kingdom.

Verse 15 tells us that the devil "spewed water like a river, to overtake the woman and sweep her away with the torrent." Some Bible scholars interpret the water literally, suggesting there will be a massive flood in Israel during the Tribulation. However, I think it is more likely that the water symbolizes some other type of aggressive assault by Satan to destroy the Jewish people through their enemies. Often in Scripture a reference to the sea can mean throngs of humanity, but it can also mean overwhelming chaos and evil.

But regardless of the form of the attack, God safeguards His own during the Tribulation, much as He protected Israel from the Egyptians during the Exodus. Believing Jews will experience His divine intervention and supernatural provision, just as they did when the Lord guided them through the wilderness.

Revelation says, "The woman was given the two wings of a great eagle" (12:14), which carry her to safety, out of reach of the evil one. Once again, God delivers and God saves. For three and a half years (the time remaining during the Tribulation), this group of Jewish believers are protected by God in the desert.

Of course the Antichrist, indwelt by Satan, will be furious that the believers have escaped his grasp, so he will send his henchmen after them. However, God will cause the earth to swallow the advancing troops.

The Antichrist will be so enraged at this counter-offensive that he will unleash his bloodiest attacks. But like his eternal destiny, the outcome of the battle has already been determined.

Jesus is victor!

Almighty God, I rejoice in Your faithfulness, Your protection, and Your provision. You are the God who saves me! All the glory and honor belong to You, for You are victorious, now and forever.

Read Revelation 12:13–17 in *The Jeremiah Study Bible*.

REVELATION 13:1–4

The dragon stood on the shore of the sea. And I saw a beast coming out of the sea. It had ten horns and seven heads, with ten crowns on its horns, and on each head a blasphemous name. The beast I saw resembled a leopard, but had feet like those of a bear and a mouth like that of a lion. The dragon gave the beast his power and his throne and great authority. One of the heads of the beast seemed to have had a fatal wound, but the fatal wound had been healed. The whole world was filled with wonder and followed the beast. People worshiped the dragon because he had given authority to the beast, and they also worshiped the beast and asked, "Who is like the beast? Who can wage war against it?"

36

MONSTER
FROM THE DEEP
(Revelation 13:1–10)

The Bible tells us that in the last days, Satan (the dragon) and the Antichrist, along with his False Prophet, will wreak havoc on the earth. They will unleash unprecedented evil and nearly endless death and destruction.

The beast that emerges from the sea in Revelation 13 is the Antichrist, the ultimate embodiment of evil. Some of what we know about this beast comes from passages in Revelation; other important details are given to us in the words of Jesus in the gospels, the prophecies of Daniel, and Paul's letters to the early Church.

Daniel 7:7–8 describes a beast with ten horns, among which a little horn rises up. This little horn has "a mouth that spoke boastfully." From this we learn that the Antichrist is persuasive, speaking "proud words and blasphemies" (Revelation 13:5). He holds the masses spellbound with his speeches and galvanizes the people of the world because of his ability to speak great things.

Daniel 7:20 says the little horn "looked more imposing than the others." So people are also attracted to the

Antichrist by his commanding appearance. Daniel 7:8 refers to the Antichrist's intellect. The Antichrist is a political and diplomatic genius. Under the guise of promoting peace, he elevates himself to a position of unparalleled power over the kingdoms of the world.

The Antichrist captures the attention of the world and accepts the worship of its people (2 Thessalonians 2:4). He speaks out against God and seeks to change "times and the laws" (Daniel 7:25). He attempts to erase all remnants of the presence of God and to elevate himself to the position of God on earth. He makes pronouncements as a deity (Revelation 13:8; 2 Thessalonians 2:4).

Satan doesn't create anything new; he only imitates or counterfeits what he sees the True Creator do. So mimicking Christ's death and resurrection, the Antichrist fakes his death and then appears to rise again.

Think what it would be like today if a great world leader were killed and then came back to life! If people thought the Antichrist was their only hope before this event, how much more will they worship him after it happens?

Just as Christ's resurrection sparked rapid growth in the Church, the so-called resurrection of the Antichrist convinces the whole world to follow him—all except for those who have come to faith in Christ, whose names have been written in the Lamb's book of life.

The Antichrist will persecute these new believers during the Tribulation. As Hitler persecuted the Jews in Germany—restricting their rights and freedoms, preventing them from engaging in commerce, publicly harassing and humiliating them, and finally torturing and murdering millions—so the Antichrist will terrorize Christians. He will wear them down with constant pressure and persecution.

These are monstrous days, calling for mammoth faith on the part of those left living on earth who want to remain true to Christ until the end.

Lord Jesus, help me remain faithful to You through my own trials and tribulations today. Fill me with compassion for the lost, that I might fearlessly make known the gospel of Christ and bring others into the family of God before the dark days to come.

Read Revelation 13:1–10 in *The Jeremiah Study Bible.*

REVELATION 13:11–13

Then I saw a second beast, coming out of the earth. It had two horns like a lamb, but it spoke like a dragon. It exercised all the authority of the first beast on its behalf, and made the earth and its inhabitants worship the first beast, whose fatal wound had been healed. And it performed great signs, even causing fire to come down from heaven to the earth in full view of the people.

37

AN UNHOLY TRINITY

(Revelation 13:11–15)

Just as the true God exists as a Trinity, Satan has an unholy trinity. His system is a counterfeit of God's, with the members of the unholy Trinity represented this way: Satan as God the Father, the Antichrist as God the Son, and the False Prophet as God the Spirit.

In John's vision in Revelation 13, he sees a beast (the Antichrist) rise out of the sea, followed by another beast rising out of the earth. This second beast is the False Prophet—the Antichrist's right-hand man and religious leader. Just as the Holy Spirit's objective is to point people to Jesus Christ, so the False Prophet's objective is to cause people to worship the Antichrist.

While the Antichrist's focus is politics, the False Prophet's emphasis is religion. During the Tribulation, with the absence of true religion, this false religion will help unite the world and solidify the political power of the Antichrist.

The False Prophet looks like a lamb—meek and mild. In reality, this leader, possessed by Satan, has the cruel heart of a serpent and the cunning voice of a dragon.

During the Tribulation, religiosity will be intense, and The False Prophet will use every counterfeit tool in his arsenal, including phony miracles that will cause the whole world to bow down to the Antichrist and worship his image.

The False Prophet will have the power to counterfeit the miracles of God. By calling down fire from heaven as Elijah did, the False Prophet will try to pass himself off as the returned Elijah of the end times (1 Kings 18:38–39; Malachi 4:5). Imagine the astonishment of all the people on earth as fire blazes across the sky! Perhaps it will be part of a gigantic celebration for the Antichrist. The False Prophet will also imitate the two witnesses, who destroyed their enemies by fire (Revelation 11:5).

Deception has been Satan's method since the beginning (Genesis 3).

The False Prophet will then convince people to build an image to worship the Antichrist and will likely set it up in the most sacred area of the Jewish temple. We aren't told what the image will be, but I believe it will be a large structure. It will become a gathering place for those coming to Jerusalem to worship the Antichrist.

Then the False Prophet will cause this image to speak! Satan cannot give life, so the image will only appear to be alive. The image will issue a decree that anyone who refuses to worship it will be killed. We don't know how this evil magic will be performed, but it is evidence of the power of demons that will prevail in those days.

Imagine the throngs of people gathering at this location every day to hear what the image has to say. The media will broadcast the image's speeches around the globe.

I believe this image is the "abomination that causes desolation" that Jesus spoke of in Matthew 24:15–18. When it is set up in Jerusalem, those who have become believers should flee to the mountains—for even greater evil is yet to come (Mark 13:14).

Lord Jesus, deliver us all from evil this day, for Yours is the kingdom, the power, and the glory forever! Amen.

Read Revelation 13:11–15 in *The Jeremiah Study Bible.*

REVELATION 13:16–18

It also forced all people, great and small, rich and poor, free and slave, to receive a mark on their right hands or on their foreheads, so that they could not buy or sell unless they had the mark, which is the name of the beast or the number of its name.

This calls for wisdom. Let the person who has insight calculate the number of the beast, for it is the number of a man. That number is 666.

38

THE MARK OF
THE BEAST
(Revelation 13:16–18)

Ruling powers usually have an identifying insignia—Nazi Germany had its swastika, the Soviet Union its hammer and sickle. The idea itself goes back to early history. Babylon was symbolized by a lion with eagle's wings (Daniel 7:4). The empire of the Medes and Persians was represented by a bear rising up with three ribs between its teeth (Daniel 7:5).

The Greek word for "mark" referred to an insignia that contained the emperor's name, effigy, and year of his reign. The mark was necessary for trade and was required on documents to attest to their validity.

The Antichrist's mark will serve the same purposes. Those without the mark will be deemed traitors and boycotted by the commercial system that the Antichrist controls.

Everyone who does not wear the mark of the beast will be denied the ability to buy or sell (Revelation 13:16–17). They will be forced to choose whether to suffer the temporary wrath of the Antichrist and receive the eternal favor of God, or to receive the temporary favor of the Antichrist and suffer the eternal wrath of God. Without access to life's basic necessities, many people will die.

Volumes have been filled with fanciful ideas and theories that attempt to describe the mark of the beast. Some think that mark will be credit cards, computer chips, barcodes, or even names of specific people. These days the idea that a government could require the world's population to carry its mark is not hard to imagine, given technological advances and widespread identification measures such as Social Security numbers and RFID chips.

No one can say exactly what form the mark of the beast will take, but the number six seems to be important (13:18). We cannot identify the exact significance of the number of the beast either. In the Bible, the number six is the number of man. Humanity was created on the sixth day and commanded to work six out of seven days. The number 666 is man's number, tripled. Six is also short of the perfect number, seven. Perhaps the number of the beast represents the ultimate opposition to God.

Whatever 666 means, and however the mark of the beast will be configured and applied during the Tribulation, it is evidence of mankind's acceptance of the Antichrist and rejection of Christ.

One thing we know for certain is that a man whose

mark is 666 will stand on the world's stage for a few moments in the future—and then face the wrath of God and be judged for all eternity.

We know that the Antichrist cannot bring history to a close. He cannot triumph. Only the one true God, through the Lord Jesus Christ, can do that.

Lord God, I choose to worship You and only You. Protect me from the enemy of my soul. Help me to see through Satan's lies and deceit, and to hold fast to the glorious truth of Your Word. All day long my hope is in You.

Read Revelation 13:16–18 in *The Jeremiah Study Bible.*

Then I looked, and there before me was the Lamb, standing on Mount Zion, and with him 144,000 who had his name and his Father's name written on their foreheads. And I heard a sound from heaven like the roar of rushing waters and like a loud peal of thunder. The sound I heard was like that of harpists playing their harps. And they sang a new song before the throne and before the four living creatures and the elders. No one could learn the song except the 144,000 who had been redeemed from the earth. These are those who did not defile themselves with women, for they remained virgins. They follow the Lamb wherever he goes. They were purchased from among mankind and offered as firstfruits to God and the Lamb.

39

BLESSED ARE
THE PURE IN HEART
(Revelation 14:1–5)

Revelation 14 is like a table of contents for the rest of the book of Revelation, chronicling the salvation of God's people, the fall of Babylon, the final battle, and God's judgment on unbelieving humanity. It contains seven visions that offer us a panoramic view of the Tribulation.

The first of these visions focuses on the Lamb of God, the central figure in the book of Revelation. We see Him slain, worshiped, feared, glorified, and now— finally—vindicated. Here, Jesus Christ, "the Lamb of God, who takes away the sin of the world" (John 1:29), stands on Mount Zion in Jerusalem with 144,000 saints who have "his Father's name written on their foreheads" (Revelation 14:1).

Mount Zion, a mountaintop in Jerusalem, was the capital city of David, the place where God's presence dwelled in the temple and the place He says He will reign forever. According to Isaiah 2:1–4, a day is coming when Mount Zion will be "the highest of the mountains," when the Law and Word of the Lord will go out from Jerusalem to the whole world. And it is at Mount Zion that the 144,000 receive their reward for completing their work.

I believe these 144,000 saints are the redeemed Jews mentioned in Revelation 7. They aren't members of the Church, the body of Christ, because the Church is already in heaven.

These 144,000 are Jewish believers representing the twelve tribes of Israel—twelve thousand from each tribe. In Revelation 7, the 144,000 had come to faith in Christ and been given the task of evangelizing the world during the Tribulation. Sealed with the mark of God on their foreheads, they were to be shielded from the enemy while they accomplished their work for the kingdom. Now Scripture reveals the rewards for their faithfulness: "Salvation belongs to our God, who sits on the throne, and to the Lamb" (7:10).

On Mount Zion, the Jewish believers are singing praises to God for fulfilling His promise to redeem them and to protect them throughout the Tribulation. Nobody else can sing their song because these witnesses are unique: only they have walked through the teeth of the Tribulation.

Blessed are the pure in heart, for they will see God. (Matthew 5:8)

One of the gross sins of the Tribulation is apostasy, what could also be described as unfaithfulness or spiritual adultery. But these witnesses remain undefiled by the world, having given themselves wholly in pure devotion to the Lord. Just as the Church is presented to Jesus as pure and innocent as a virgin (2 Corinthians 11:2), so these believers remain "virgins"—pure in heart and in ministry.

The Scripture tells us many people will be saved as a result of their preaching.

Clearly, there is no power like that of people who have kept themselves pure from the world and who have God's seal upon them, ready to stand apart and preach to a generation!

Lord Jesus, cleanse me with Your blood and make me holy and pure of heart today. I offer You all that I am and all that I ever will be, for Your service and Your glory.

Read Revelation 14:1–5 in *The Jeremiah Study Bible*.

Then I saw another angel flying in midair, and he had the eternal gospel to proclaim to those who live on the earth—to every nation, tribe, language and people. He said in a loud voice, "Fear God and give him glory, because the hour of his judgment has come. Worship him who made the heavens, the earth, the sea and the springs of water."

A second angel followed and said, "'Fallen! Fallen is Babylon the Great,' which made all the nations drink the maddening wine of her adulteries."

A third angel followed them and said in a loud voice: "If anyone worships the beast and its image and receives its mark on their forehead or on their hand, they, too, will drink the wine of God's fury, which has been poured full strength into the cup of his wrath. They will be tormented with burning sulfur in the presence of the holy angels and of the Lamb.

40

ONE LAST CHANCE
(Revelation 14:6–13)

In Greek drama, important scenes weren't always enacted on the stage. Instead, a messenger would come onstage and announce that a battle, riot, or other significant event had taken place. This is the role of the six angels of Revelation 14. These angels announce the events in prophetic history that will affect the people of God who are still living on earth during the Tribulation.

The first angel is described in 14:6–7. He declares the everlasting gospel. How appropriate it is that during this dark time, when mankind will be worshiping the beast and his image, one last attempt is made to call people to worship the true God. Even in the midst of judgment, God continues to offer His mercy and grace.

The second angel announces that Babylon is "fallen" (14:8). The mention of Babylon signals the final overthrow of the false religious system of the end times. Most scholars believe that Babylon refers not only to a city but also to the idolatrous worship that centers on Satan (17:2). The repetition of the word *fallen* underscores the certainty of its destruction.

The third angel announces the options of those dwelling on earth: they can choose to worship the beast and be judged by God, or they can choose to worship God and be judged by the beast (14:9–12). There is no other choice. In the ultimate battle of good and evil, there is no neutral ground, no compromise.

The torment for those who choose to worship the beast will last forever, but the torment for those who refuse him will only last a little while—and then they will experience peace, joy, and glory forever! For this reason, in Revelation 14:12, the angel calls believers to have "patient endurance."

We come now to one of the greatest passages in all of Scripture—a promise to those who endure the Tribulation and are granted "rest from their labor" (14:13). The Greek word for "rest" pictures world-weary sailors who have spent their lives at sea and finally come to their home port. The word means "refreshment, renewal, and rejuvenation," or "the absence of struggle and persecution."

Those who respond to the gospel preached by the 144,000 will be saved during the Tribulation and will have access to Bibles, Christian books, and biblical sermons and messages that have been left behind after the Rapture. These saints are too many to number (7:9). God gives this promise to them to ease their minds about their future rewards: "Blessed are the dead who die in the Lord from now on" (14:13). If they die during the Tribulation—too late for the Rapture and too early for the kingdom—they will still be blessed. They will still find their way to their eternal home with Him.

Heavenly Father, I lift my voice in praise that even in the midst of judgment, You continue to extend Your grace and mercy to mankind. What a comfort it is to know that while there is life, there is hope— and even in death, there is hope! One by one, You will bring us all safely home.

Read Revelation 14:6–13 in *The Jeremiah Study Bible.*

REVELATION 14:14–16

I looked, and there before me was a white cloud, and seated on the cloud was one like a son of man with a crown of gold on his head and a sharp sickle in his hand. Then another angel came out of the temple and called in a loud voice to him who was sitting on the cloud, "Take your sickle and reap, because the time to reap has come, for the harvest of the earth is ripe." So he who was seated on the cloud swung his sickle over the earth, and the earth was harvested.

41

A HORRIFYING HARVEST

(Revelation 14:14–20)

A holocaust, the likes of which the world has never seen, is coming upon this earth. It's the battle to end all battles: Armageddon.

As many as two hundred million people will gather in the land of Israel on the plain of Megiddo. The amount of blood that will be shed at this last battle is staggering: it has the proportions of a flood, covering about two-hundred-miles and reaching a depth of approximately four feet. According to Ezekiel, seven years will be required to rid the earth of the weapons that have been accumulated by the nations, and seven months will be required to bury the dead (Ezekiel 39:8–16).

It's hard to imagine, really.

But once again, in Revelation 14, we see the dichotomy between the false and the true, the real and the counterfeit. Satan is an angel of light and a master counterfeiter, doing everything he can to blind people's eyes and close their ears to the gospel, leading them to believe lies rather than the truth.

In John 15, see how Jesus describes Himself:

I am the vine; you are the branches. If you remain in me and I in you, you will bear much fruit; apart from me you can do nothing. If you do not remain in me, you are like a branch that is thrown away and withers; such branches are picked up, thrown into the fire and burned. If you remain in me and my words remain in you, ask whatever you wish, and it will be done for you. This is to my Father's glory, that you bear much fruit, showing yourselves to be my disciples. (vv. 15:5–8)

Now, according to Revelation 14:18, Satan, too, functions like a vine, to which his followers are attached. But the fruit they produce is rotten. It's the fruit of wickedness. The people of the earth are as clusters of grapes, ripe and ready to be harvested. They will be cut off and thrown into the winepress of God's wrath.

It's important to know that this is no random harvest. Using another reaping metaphor, Matthew shows us that Jesus carefully gathers all the "wheat," keeping it separate from the "tares" (weeds).

As the weeds are pulled up and burned in the fire, so it will be at the end of the age. The Son of Man will send out his angels, and they will weed out of his kingdom everything that causes sin and all who do evil. They will throw them into the blazing furnace, where there will be weeping and gnashing of teeth. Then the righteous will shine like the sun in the kingdom of their Father. (Matthew 13:40–43)

Jesus, the Lord of the harvest, thoroughly supervises the separation work done by the angels so that no believer is judged with the unbelievers. And immediately afterward, He triumphantly returns to earth, bringing an end to the Tribulation.

Lord Jesus, You are holy and just in all Your ways. Protect me from the enemy of my soul today and keep me from being deceived. Help me to see clearly and hold fast to Your Truth.

Read Revelation 14:14–20 in *The Jeremiah Study Bible.*

REVELATION 15:1–3

I saw in heaven another great and marvelous sign: seven angels with the seven last plagues— last, because with them God's wrath is completed. And I saw what looked like a sea of glass glowing with fire and, standing beside the sea, those who had been victorious over the beast and its image and over the number of its name. They held harps given them by God and sang the song of God's servant Moses and of the Lamb:

> *"Great and marvelous are your deeds,*
>> *Lord God Almighty.*
> *Just and true are your ways,*
>> *King of the nations."*

42

THE HARD TRUTH
(Revelation 15:1–8)

Let's face it: no one likes to contemplate the terrible events described in Revelation. But ignoring them won't make them less likely to occur. Perhaps the most helpful way to approach them is to ask whether judgment is consistent with the character of God.

In our generation we have lost sight of the holiness of God. We have forgotten His justice, His righteousness. "Consider therefore the kindness and sternness of God" (Romans 11:22).

Throughout recorded history God has been expressing His loving-kindness and extending His mercy and grace to mankind. Even during the Tribulation, He shows again and again that His heart is to be reconciled with all He has created.

In the end, those who are judged are the people who have stubbornly, utterly refused Him. They have made it clear that *they do not want His forgiveness.* They do not want mercy or grace, even when it is offered to them. And so, finally, He takes them at their word.

The word *plagues* in Revelation 15:1 is translated elsewhere as "wounds." The Lord is about to wound the earth for the last time before the final judgment. There is a company of saints who became Christians during the Tribulation. They have refused to take the mark of the beast and resisted the temptation to worship him. And their victory, which led to their martyrdom, has resulted in their entrance into heaven.

The Tribulation saints sing something called "the song of God's servant Moses" (15:3; Deuteronomy 32). This song depicts the retribution and justice God serves His enemies and reveals the greatness of His works, His ways, His worth, and His worship (Romans 11:33).

The saints also sing the "song . . . of the Lamb" (Revelation 15:3).

The phrase, "I looked, and I saw," signifies something new that hasn't been seen before (15:5). John sees the Holy of Holies in the heavenly temple. In Old Testament times, only the high priest could enter the Holy of Holies in the temple, and only on the Day of Atonement. He would offer the blood sacrifice on the mercy seat to satisfy God's justice against sin for another year. Seeing the angels coming from the Holy of Holies reminds us that judgment flows from the holiness of God. In Revelation 15:8, the temple is filled with smoke from the glory of God. In the Bible, smoke often symbolizes the presence and glory of the Lord.

The hard truth is this: those who refuse to drink the

cup of God's salvation must drink from the bowls of His wrath (Psalm 75:8).

If you're already a believer, you won't be on earth during the seven bowl judgments. So why does all of this concern you?

Think about it: if Jesus Christ came back today, the events described in Revelation 15–16 would happen seven years from now. Do you know anyone who will still be alive in seven years? Do they know Christ as their Savior? If the Rapture occurred today, would they be left behind on the earth to endure the seven bowl judgments?

Lord Jesus, today I recommit to pray for friends and loved ones who don't yet know You as their Savior. Give me the courage, the sensitivity, and the opportunity to share Your gospel with them before it's too late!

Read Revelation 15:1–8 in *The Jeremiah Study Bible*.

Then I heard a loud voice from the temple saying to the seven angels, "Go, pour out the seven bowls of God's wrath on the earth."

The first angel went and poured out his bowl on the land, and ugly, festering sores broke out on the people who had the mark of the beast and worshiped its image.

The second angel poured out his bowl on the sea, and it turned into blood like that of a dead person, and every living thing in the sea died.

The third angel poured out his bowl on the rivers and springs of water, and they became blood. . . .

The fourth angel poured out his bowl on the sun, and the sun was allowed to scorch people with fire. . . .

The fifth angel poured out his bowl on the throne of the beast, and its kingdom was plunged into darkness. . . .

The sixth angel poured out his bowl on the great river Euphrates, and its water was dried up to prepare the way for the kings from the East. . . .

The seventh angel poured out his bowl into the air, and out of the temple came a loud voice from the throne, saying, "It is done!"

43

A CATASTROPHIC CONCLUSION

(Revelation 16:1–21)

I t's the beginning of the end for the "late great planet earth." In Revelation 16, we learn of the last judgments—the bowl judgments—that will be executed at the very end of the Tribulation, right before Christ's triumphant return.

Just when it looked like it couldn't get any worse!

God commands the seven angels to pour out the seven bowls of His wrath upon the earth, each one in turn. Many of these judgments are reminiscent of the plagues He sent on the Egyptians in Exodus.

When the first angel pours out his bowl, "ugly, festering sores broke out on the people who had the mark of the beast" (16:2). They now bear the mark of God's judgment, an outward sign of their inner corruption.

The second angel pours out his bowl, and the sea turns to blood (16:3). Every living creature in the sea dies.

The third angel pours his bowl on the rivers, and they, too, "became blood" (16:4). The angel observes that this is a just punishment, "for they have shed the blood of your holy people and your prophets, and you have given them blood to drink as they deserve" (16:5–6). The martyrs gathered around the altar add their amen: "Yes, Lord God Almighty, true and just are your judgments" (16:7).

The fourth angel unleashes the power of the sun to scorch humanity "with fire" (16:8). But even as people gnaw their tongues with pain from the sores and suffer from thirst and intense heat, they continue to curse God and refuse to repent.

The fifth angel pours out his bowl on the throne of the Antichrist, and the world is plunged in darkness (16:10). This outer darkness reflects the world's dark heart and soul.

The sixth angel pours out his bowl, and the Euphrates River dries up. This makes way for the kings of the earth and their armies to cross over and gather for the Battle of Armageddon (16:12). Then John describes seeing three evil spirits that look like frogs "go out to the kings of the whole world," provoking, deceiving, and manipulating them until they're all enraged and ready go to war "on the great day of God Almighty" (16:14). Satan has one purpose: utter destruction of God's people. He wants to destroy Israel God's beloved people and defeat His kingdom, His plans, and His purposes for the earth.

The seventh and final bowl judgment brings the Tribulation to its catastrophic conclusion. The seventh angel tips his bowl into the air, and the words, "It is done!" ring out from the temple (16:17), reminding us of Jesus's words on the cross (John 19:30).

As Revelation 16 concludes, suddenly the world is rocked by thunder, lightning, and a "severe earthquake" (16:18). The biggest earthquake in history splits the city apart, causing it to fall to pieces and collapse. The surrounding nations also suffer the same devastation. It's the beginning of the final destruction of every religious, political, and educational institution that humanity has built apart from God.

Almighty God, this chapter is a sobering reminder of the utter devastation sin brings and the judgment we all deserve. Thank You for sending Jesus to rescue me from this. Thank You for Your mercy and grace. Help me walk humbly before You all of my days.

Read Revelation 16:1–21 in *The Jeremiah Study Bible.*

REVELATION 17:1–2, 5–6

One of the seven angels who had the seven bowls came and said to me, "Come, I will show you the punishment of the great prostitute, who sits by many waters. With her the kings of the earth committed adultery, and the inhabitants of the earth were intoxicated with the wine of her adulteries." . . .

The name written on her forehead was a mystery:

BABYLON THE GREAT
THE MOTHER OF PROSTITUTES
AND OF THE ABOMINATIONS
OF THE EARTH.

I saw that the woman was drunk with the blood of God's holy people, the blood of those who bore testimony to Jesus.

44

AN END TO
AN UNFAITHFUL CHURCH
(Revelation 17:1–18)

The Scripture tells us that in the end times, people will flock to a counterfeit version of Christianity—a cult that twists and perverts the faith. Adherents of the devil's spiritually adulterous system only *appear* to worship the one true God. In reality, their hearts are far from Him.

This false church is described as a the "great prostitute" (17:1) because she commits spiritual adultery by joining herself to the Antichrist and worshiping him. Any worship besides the worship of God is spiritual adultery—it is idolatry and unfaithfulness. It cannot go unjudged.

The harlotry of the false religious system is seen in her easy alliance with the political powers of the world. The seven heads and ten horns speak of the political system of the beast, the Antichrist. The unfaithful woman (the false church) and the beast agree to combine their powers and take over the West.

This "great prostitute" is dressed like a queen: clothing of purple and scarlet, adorned with gold, precious stones, and pearls. But the golden cup she holds is full of "abominable things and the filth of her adulteries" (17:4). This is the way sin works; it comes covered in an attractive veneer that hides its evil and hideous consequences.

John is no doubt shocked to discover that the woman is drunk with the blood of the saints. He might have expected the pagan Roman Empire to torture and kill Christians because he had seen this firsthand, in his own lifetime. Remember he writes the book of Revelation from a place of exile, where he is being punished for preaching the gospel. But he is "greatly astonished" (17:6) to see what appears to be the church participating in the slaughter of true believers.

God, however, is just, and He will not allow her wickedness to go unpunished. The blood of the martyrs must be avenged. In a dramatic turn of events, the false church is betrayed by the beast and suffers a horrific fate.

In Revelation 17:12–14, we learn there are ten kings who will be given authority to rule the world along with the Antichrist during the Tribulation. They bring the prostitute to ruin—they despise her, consume her, and ultimately destroy her.

Then they will wage war against the Lamb of God, "but the Lamb will triumph over them because he is Lord of lords and King of kings" (17:14).

Prophetic events cast long shadows. We learn from this that the Church today must not look to politics or the state to form partnerships that promise us earthly power. We must be vigilant to maintain a pure, unadulterated gospel, free of distortion, corruption, and idolatry. And we must make sure we remain holy, set apart for God, and separate from the world.

To give up a relationship with Christ for anyone or anything else is madness.

Jesus Christ, show me how to walk in love, in purity, and in faithfulness to Your Word. Keep me from being deceived by the enemy of my soul or tempted by worldly pleasure or power. Help me to stand fast and hold on to Your Truth.

Read Revelation 17:1–18 in *The Jeremiah Study Bible.*

After this I saw another angel coming down from heaven. He had great authority, and the earth was illuminated by his splendor. With a mighty voice he shouted:

"'Fallen! Fallen is Babylon the Great!'

She has become a dwelling for demons and a haunt for every impure spirit,

a haunt for every unclean bird,

a haunt for every unclean and detestable animal.

For all the nations have drunk

the maddening wine of her adulteries.

The kings of the earth committed adultery with her,

and the merchants of the earth grew rich from her excessive luxuries."

Then I heard another voice from heaven say:

"'Come out of her, my people,'

so that you will not share in her sins,

so that you will not receive any of her plagues."

45

ASHES TO ASHES
(Revelation 18:1–24)

In his miraculous vision, John sees an angel whose splendor illuminates the earth (18:1). This angel prophesies the cataclysmic destruction of Babylon: "Fallen! Fallen is Babylon the Great!" (18:2).

It was once considered the most luxurious, enlightened, and liberated city on the planet, having given free rein to every form of immorality and depravity. But in a single hour, the magnificence of Babylon—in all her religious, political, and economic glory—will be reduced to an ash heap, destroyed by One with greater authority and glory (18:10).

The loss of this capital of sin causes the leaders of the world to weep, as much for their loss as for hers. They've relied on Babylon for their success and well-being, and now everything is gone. Because they benefit financially from Babylon's power, the merchants and mariners of the earth also mourn when the economic hub of the world is destroyed. Indeed, the people of the earth weep and wail and lament the destruction of the great city in which they had put their hope.

Perhaps what is most striking, though, is what they do *not* mourn—their sin.

They're grieved to lose their lifestyle, their wealth, their society, their safety and security. But they have brought it on themselves.

Babylon's sins "are piled up to heaven, and God has remembered her crimes" (18:5). The Greek word "piled" means "to come in contact with." The city's sins are so vast, they touch the heavens (an allusion to the Tower of Babel in Genesis 11). One of their greatest sins is their inhumanity—their treatment of other human beings as commodities to be bought and sold and enslaved (18:13). Now they face God's wrath.

An angel hurls a boulder into the sea as a symbol of the violence of their destruction (18:21). The city that caused so many in the world to stumble has a figurative millstone placed around her neck before she is cast into the sea of God's judgment.

Notice the word *never* is used five times in 18:21–23. Never, *ever* again will human joys exist in Babylon. What a picture of final desolation! When God judges, His judgment is sure and final.

So how should we, as believers, respond to the judgment and fall of Babylon?

The voice John hears from heaven says it plainly: "'Come out of her, my people,' so that you will not share in her sins, so that you will not receive any of her plagues" (18:4).

It echoes the words of 2 Corinthians 6:17: "Come out from them and be separate, says the Lord." And this: "For God did not call us to be impure, but to live a holy life" (1 Thessalonians 4:7).

And 1 Thessalonians 3:13 adds, "May he strengthen your hearts so that you will be blameless and holy in the presence of our God and Father when our Lord Jesus comes with all his holy ones."

Lord Jesus, as I reflect on the destruction that awaits those who revel in their sin, I want more than ever to "come out from them and be separate." Show me how to keep my heart and life pure. Make me holy, even as You are holy, for Your glory and Your name's sake.

Read Revelation 18:1–24 in *The Jeremiah Study Bible*.

REVELATION 19:6–8

*Then I heard what sounded like a great multitude,
like the roar of rushing waters and like loud peals
of thunder, shouting:*
  "Hallelujah!
    For our Lord God Almighty reigns.
  Let us rejoice and be glad
    and give him glory!
  For the wedding of the Lamb has come,
    and his bride has made herself ready.
  Fine linen, bright and clean,
    was given her to wear."

46

HERE COMES THE BRIDE

(Revelation 19:1–10)

R evelation tells us that the angels, the Old Testament saints, the Church saints, and the Tribulation saints will one day raise their voices in a choir that will reverberate more powerfully than any other choir in the history of the world.

"Hallelujah! Salvation and glory and power belong to our God . . . Amen, Hallelujah!" (19:1, 4).

This great hallelujah chorus is the prelude to the marriage of the Bridegroom to His Bride, the Church.

In the first century, weddings took place in three stages, from a couple's betrothal to their union in marriage. First, the parents of the bride and the bridegroom negotiated a marriage contract. From this point on, the couple would be considered legally married, though there would be no intimate contact for years to come. The second step took place when the bridegroom, accompanied by his friends, came to the bride's house to bring her back to the new home he had been preparing for them. Usually this home was an annex or suite of rooms added onto the family home—his father's house.

The bridal party would make their way there in a grand procession, which was followed by a marriage feast that could last for days.

In the same way, we as believers in Jesus "legally" entered into a marriage to Christ at the time we first trusted in Him. Now we, as the Bride, are waiting for our Bridegroom to come and take us to the home He has prepared for us in His Father's house, where the wedding of the Lamb will take place. This will occur at the Rapture of the Church. Together, we will then celebrate the marriage supper of the Lamb on earth, after the Second Coming.

> Do not let your hearts be troubled. You believe in God; believe also in me. My Father's house has many rooms; if that were not so, would I have told you that I am going there to prepare a place for you? And if I go and prepare a place for you, I will come back and take you to be with me that you also may be where I am. (John 14:1–3)

The bridal party includes not only the Bride (the Church) but also the companions of the Bride and the companions of the Bridegroom. I believe the latter include the resurrected Old Testament saints (Daniel 12:2) and the redeemed of Israel, miraculously converted during the Tribulation. This marriage feast is a magnificent redemptive meal celebrating the uniting of Jews and Gentiles into one body, married to the head of the body, Jesus Christ.

In Bible times, the length of the marriage supper depended on the wealth of the family hosting the feast. Since our heavenly Father owns it all, this marriage feast will last for a thousand years!

But unlike weddings of the last century, the center of attraction will not be the Bride, but the Bridegroom—Jesus Christ. It's His beauty we will praise, His glory we will share.

Jesus, I'm so honored to be a part of the Church, Your Bride. How I long to be in Your presence, celebrating the love we share for all eternity. Help me be ready for Your return and our glorious wedding day!

Read Revelation 19:1–10 in *The Jeremiah Study Bible*.

REVELATION 19:11–16

I saw heaven standing open and there before me was a white horse, whose rider is called Faithful and True. With justice he judges and wages war. His eyes are like blazing fire, and on his head are many crowns. He has a name written on him that no one knows but he himself. He is dressed in a robe dipped in blood, and his name is the Word of God. The armies of heaven were following him, riding on white horses and dressed in fine linen, white and clean. Coming out of his mouth is a sharp sword with which to strike down the nations. "He will rule them with an iron scepter." He treads the winepress of the fury of the wrath of God Almighty. On his robe and on his thigh he has this name written:

KING OF KINGS AND
LORD OF LORDS.

47

THE BEST DAY EVER

(Revelation 19:11–16)

From the Old Testament prophets to present-day believers, God's people have desperately longed for the moment they would see Jesus return to establish His kingdom of peace and justice on the earth.

The Bible is filled with references to the Second Coming of Christ. This spectacular event is emphasized in seventeen Old Testament books, and 70 percent of the chapters of the New Testament make reference to it. Christ Himself said He would return, as did the angels who spoke to those who witnessed His ascension.

In John's vision in Revelation 19:11, the door to heaven opens for the second time. The first time, Jesus caught up the saints with Him in the Rapture (4:1). The second time, He is riding a white stallion, a symbolic picture of conquest—appearing the same way a victorious king would reenter the capital city of his kingdom after battle in ancient times. And this time He will be accompanied by us, His people: "For he has rescued us from the dominion of darkness and brought us into the kingdom" (Colossians 1:13).

At His first coming, Jesus was the Lamb who came

to take away the sins of the world. But at His Second Coming, He will restore truth and righteousness and execute just judgment on His enemies. How exciting it is to know that we will be a part of the vast army that returns with Him!

The Bible tells us that this Second Coming of Christ will be a glorious event that all the world will witness. It won't be a secret or a purely spiritual experience subject to question or debate. Everyone—believers and unbelievers alike—will know when it has happened. And it will happen suddenly—like the lightning that begins in the east and shines to the west (Matthew 24:27–30).

As this scene opens in Revelation 19:11, all the nations are gathered for a final assault against God and His people. But this battle is unlike any other in history. The outcome of the battle is never in doubt. And the army of the saints never even lift a hand—let alone a sword.

Christ simply comes down and with His Word slays His enemies. With a shout of praise, the battle is over before it even begins.

Revelation 19 uses three names to refer to Christ: The first, "Faithful and True," indicates His oneness with the Father and thus His eternal existence (19:11). The second name, the "Word of God" (19:13), refers to Jesus's incarnation, when the "Word became flesh" (John 1:14). The third, "KING OF KINGS AND LORD OF

LORDS" (19:16), is the title Christ will have in His role as the sovereign ruler of the earth (Isaiah 9:6–7).

On that great day, Scripture tells us, at the name of Jesus, every knee will bow, in heaven and on earth and under the earth, and every tongue will confess that He is Lord (Philippians 2:11).

What a privilege it will be to share that day— to experience it together with Him!

What a privilege it is to declare our love and allegiance to Him now!

King of kings and Lord of Lords, I worship and adore You! I live today—and every day—in eager anticipation of Your triumphant and glorious return. Hallelujah! Come, Lord Jesus!

Read Revelation 19:11–16 in *The Jeremiah Study Bible.*

And I saw an angel standing in the sun, who cried in a loud voice to all the birds flying in midair, "Come, gather together for the great supper of God, so that you may eat the flesh of kings, generals, and the mighty, of horses and their riders, and the flesh of all people, free and slave, great and small."

Then I saw the beast and the kings of the earth and their armies gathered together to wage war against the rider on the horse and his army. But the beast was captured, and with it the false prophet who had performed the signs on its behalf. With these signs he had deluded those who had received the mark of the beast and worshiped its image. The two of them were thrown alive into the fiery lake of burning sulfur. The rest were killed with the sword coming out of the mouth of the rider on the horse, and all the birds gorged themselves on their flesh.

48

A MEAL YOU WANT TO MISS

(Revelation 19:17–21)

It's thrilling to know that each one of us has been invited to the marriage supper of the Lamb, a time of great rejoicing and celebration! Anyone and everyone who has trusted in Christ will be there. At the same time, it's sobering to realize that millions of unrepentant followers of the Antichrist and the False Prophet will find their presence is required at an entirely different kind of banquet, "the great supper of God" (19:17). At this supper, there will be no rejoicing, only weeping and wailing. Those who managed to survive the horrors of the Tribulation and still choose to reject Christ will become food for the vultures on the battlefield of Armageddon.

Revelation tells us that the Antichrist and his followers gather one last time to try to defeat Jesus Christ. All the evil and rebellion of the previous seven years comes to a head at the Battle of Armageddon.

But the battle is over as soon as it's begun. Immediately, the Antichrist and the False Prophet are captured. The Antichrist and the False Prophet find themselves face-to-face with the Righteous Judge, the Lord Jesus Christ. Their evil acts have been so numerous and so monstrous that they are thrown alive into the "fiery lake of burning sulfur" (19:20). The Antichrist and the False Prophet become the first inhabitants of the final hell. Both will still be there after a thousand years, when the first member of the unholy trinity, Satan, joins them (20:10). The Antichrist's armies are killed by the conquering Christ; their bodies will be consumed by scavengers while their souls are sent to Hades to await the Great White Throne Judgment (20:11–15).

In light of biblical prophecies like these, we can't afford to be careless about our own relationship with Christ—or callous about the horrific events in store for many of our fellow human beings.

> Since everything will be destroyed in this way, what kind of people ought you to be? You ought to live holy and godly lives as you look forward to the day of God and speed its coming. (2 Peter 3:11–12)

We should be motivated by compassion for those who do not know Christ and do everything we can to depopulate hell by sharing the gospel with them, bringing them into the family of God.

If the task seems too overwhelming, consider taking a small step: invite a neighbor, coworker, friend, or family member to church. Better yet, invite them into your home, open your heart to them, really listen to them, and look for opportunities to respectfully share the reason for the hope within you (1 Peter 3:15).

Or simply start by praying faithfully for one person to hear and receive the gospel before it's too late.

Lord Jesus, as I look forward to Your return, fill me with love and compassion for the lost. Show me what I can do to bring them to You.

Read Revelation 19:17–21 in *The Jeremiah Study Bible.*

REVELATION 20:1–5

And I saw an angel coming down out of heaven, having the key to the Abyss and holding in his hand a great chain. He seized the dragon, that ancient serpent, who is the devil, or Satan, and bound him for a thousand years. He threw him into the Abyss, and locked and sealed it over him, to keep him from deceiving the nations anymore until the thousand years were ended. After that, he must be set free for a short time.

I saw thrones on which were seated those who had been given authority to judge. And I saw the souls of those who had been beheaded because of their testimony about Jesus and because of the word of God. They had not worshiped the beast or its image and had not received its mark on their foreheads or their hands. They came to life and reigned with Christ a thousand years. (The rest of the dead did not come to life until the thousand years were ended.) This is the first resurrection.

49

WHAT KIND OF
MILLENNIAL ARE YOU?
(Revelation 20:1–5)

Millennium means "one thousand years." Revelation 20 contains the only specific New Testament references to the Millennium. In the Bible, it refers to the period when Christ will rule as King over all the earth from His capital, Jerusalem. He will set right all that the enemy has perverted and destroyed since creation (1 John 3:8).

The saints of God, who return with Him for the Battle of Armageddon, will also rule from the New Jerusalem, helping to oversee a thousand years of peace and righteousness on earth while Satan is imprisoned in the Abyss. "They came to life and reigned with Christ a thousand years" (Revelation 20:4).

Just when and how all of this will take place is a controversial issue among Christians. But the Millennium is such an important theme in John's narrative of Revelation that he mentions it six times. We should know where we stand.

A *premillennialist* believes that Christ will return to earth before the Millennium begins. He will then establish

His kingdom and set up His throne in Jerusalem. God's promises to the descendants of Abraham, Isaac, and Jacob will be kept as an unconditional covenant. Most evangelicals take a premillennialist position.

A *postmillennialist* believes the world will get better and this present time will become the age of the Millennium. This optimism was especially popular during the nineteenth and twentieth centuries. Then came World War I, the Great Depression, the rise of Hitler, World War II, and more "wars and rumors of wars" (Matthew 24:6). The view that believers can bring about utopia by setting a godly example has faded.

An *amillennialist* does not believe there will be a literal thousand-year reign of peace on earth. Amillennialists believe the Church is the fulfillment of the kingdom and that Christ reigns today through believers in peace and righteousness.

There are faithful Christians who hold to each of these three views. We should never use a person's view on the Millennium as a test of fellowship or orthodoxy. But it's important to establish a scriptural foundation for our own view.

You might be wondering, *Why do we need a Millennium at all? Why don't we just jump from here to eternity in heaven?*

The Scriptures explain that the Millennium is a glorious reward for the faithful, God's people who will reign together with Christ over the earth (Matthew 16:27). We've read in the book of Revelation about the devastation of our planet during the Tribulation. It's in the Millennium that creation will be redeemed. The earth will be made new and beautiful once more.

Another reason for the Millennium? It shows us mankind's depravity. At the end of the "thousand years," Satan will hold sway one last time. People will listen to his lies, fall for his schemes, and willingly carry out his evil deeds. A perfect environment doesn't prevent sin from taking place.

It's only the blood of Jesus that can break the curse and set us free from our old nature. It's only the saving grace of Jesus that can redeem us, restore us, and make us new.

Lord Jesus, You alone are the Prince of Peace. You rule with justice; You reign with righteousness, forever and ever. Reign in me today.

Read Revelation 20:1–5 in *The Jeremiah Study Bible*.

REVELATION 20:6

Blessed and holy are those who share in the first resurrection. The second death has no power over them, but they will be priests of God and of Christ and will reign with him for a thousand years.

50

IN A PERFECT WORLD

(Revelation 20:6)

Many of us talk about what we imagine life could be "in a perfect world." Some of us even wonder what might have been if not for the fall of Adam and Eve back in Genesis 3. The book of Revelation tells us a day is coming when we will experience a truly perfect world, a thousand years of peace and righteousness here on earth. The Old Testament prophets were often given glimpses of Christ's kingdom, which they described for us, giving us many hints of things to come.

There will be countless blessings and benefits of living during the Millennium. It helps to think of them as falling into five categories emphasized in Scripture:

1. *It will be a time of peace.* This is when the prophecy about beating swords into plowshares will finally come true (Micah 4:3). There will be no more war or rumors of war. Even the members of the animal kingdom will live in peace with one another and with people (Isaiah 11:6). Fear will be a thing of the past, and there will be nothing but good news to report, day after day.

2. *It will be a time of prosperity.* There will be no drought, no famine, no failed harvests (Isaiah 35:1–10). Every land will flourish, well-watered and fruitful. Every person will prosper.

3. *It will be a time of purity.* When a king who is holy is ruling, that influence of holiness tends to extend to every part of his kingdom (Isaiah 25:9). With Christ as King, holiness will pervade the earth. All people will worship God and pursue righteousness.

4. *It will be a time of perpetual health.* There will be no more sickness or disease, no more mental illness or addiction, no more birth defects, and no more deterioration that comes with age. Children will be born abundantly, and the population will increase rapidly and fill the earth.

5. *It will be a time of personal joy.* A deep-seated joy that flows from a clear conscience will fill the earth when God is reigning over all. People will no longer live in selfishness or self-loathing. The consequences of sin, the pain, agony, and despair that so often characterize our world today, will be replaced by the joy of the Lord.

During his vision of the thousand-year reign of Christ, John sees thrones and a group of people sitting on them who are given the authority to judge. The apostle Paul explained to the Corinthians that the saints would judge the world and even judge angels (1 Corinthians 6:2–3). These people are those dead in Christ, the believers who were caught up during the Rapture, and the Tribulation saints.

A perfect world is more than a pipe dream. It's something we can all look forward to, a time of peace on earth for "those on whom his favor rests" (Luke 2:14).

Lord, may Your peace rule in my heart today, even as I prepare for that day when Your glorious kingdom is established here on earth and Your perfect peace rules over all.

Read Revelation 20:6 in *The Jeremiah Study Bible.*

REVELATION 20:7–10

When the thousand years are over, Satan will be released from his prison and will go out to deceive the nations in the four corners of the earth— Gog and Magog—and to gather them for battle. In number they are like the sand on the seashore. They marched across the breadth of the earth and surrounded the camp of God's people, the city he loves. But fire came down from heaven and devoured them. And the devil, who deceived them, was thrown into the lake of burning sulfur, where the beast and the false prophet had been thrown. They will be tormented day and night for ever and ever.

51

A PAINFUL
REALITY CHECK
(Revelation 20:7–10)

For thousands of years, Satan has deceived people into thinking they can find a way to build a world of peace and love *without Christ*. Some are convinced that the key is education or equality or a strong government or a secure economy. Others say, "If only we could all just try to be more tolerant, more understanding of one another . . ."

But our sin nature—not only aided and abetted, but prodded and provoked by Satan—has made it impossible. The reality is that the world's problems can never be solved, and peace cannot be established apart from the saving grace of the Prince of Peace, Jesus Christ.

Revelation tells us that at the appointed time before the Millennium begins, an angel will come down from heaven, seize Satan, bind him for a thousand years, and throw him into a bottomless pit. There the devil will be contained, with a seal placed over him, so that he cannot continue to tempt, deceive, "steal and kill and destroy" (John 10:10).

During the Millennium, believers will be free from

the evil influence and harassment of Satan. They will populate the earth, living in an ideal environment, with King Jesus as their loving, benevolent ruler. But the startling truth is that their offspring—who have only known a perfect world of peace and love—can still choose to rebel against God . . . and some will.

Satan will be released and allowed to wreak havoc one more time. He will gather some of his old cohorts—the nations that hated Israel—and march on Jerusalem once more. People will actually volunteer to be part of his army to attack Jerusalem, the city of Christ and His saints.

This battle will not last long, for fire will come down from heaven and consume them. After his armies are destroyed, Satan will be thrown "into the lake of burning sulfur, where the beast and the false prophet had been thrown. They will be tormented day and night for ever and ever" (20:10). The final judgment of the unholy trinity introduced in chapters 12 and 13 will be complete.

Many believers reading the book of Revelation have struggled to understand why God would give Satan another chance to do his worst. Why, once he has been bound and gagged, would God would allow Satan to come back and stir up trouble again? Why not be done with him?

But it seems that this is part of God's plan to help us

understand that even if we are raised in a perfect world of peace and love, under the most ideal conditions imaginable, the human heart is still "deceitful above all things and beyond cure" (Jeremiah 17:9). Given a chance, and left to its own devices, it will always choose depravity.

It is only by God's mercy and grace that any of us is saved. It is only through the shed blood of Jesus, and His Spirit working in us and through us, that we have the power to resist the evil one and the evil within.

Lord, thank You for rescuing me from the power of sin. Help me walk in humility, in grace, in gratitude, and in love for You all of my days.

Read Revelation 20:7–10 in *The Jeremiah Study Bible*.

REVELATION 20:11–15

Then I saw a great white throne and him who was seated on it. The earth and the heavens fled from his presence, and there was no place for them. And I saw the dead, great and small, standing before the throne, and books were opened. Another book was opened, which is the book of life. The dead were judged according to what they had done as recorded in the books. The sea gave up the dead that were in it, and death and Hades gave up the dead that were in them, and each person was judged according to what they had done. Then death and Hades were thrown into the lake of fire. The lake of fire is the second death. Anyone whose name was not found written in the book of life was thrown into the lake of fire.

52

JUSTICE IS SERVED
Revelation 20:11–15

The Bible tells us that all people are "destined to die once, and after that to face judgment" (Hebrews 9:27). One day everyone who has ever lived will be called to stand before the Righteous Judge of the earth. But we won't all have the same court date. Nor will the purpose of our hearing—or the end result—be the same.

The New Testament describes at least three future judgments: The *Judgment Seat of Christ* occurs after the Rapture, while the Church is in heaven during the seven-year Tribulation on earth (2 Corinthians 5:10). This is when faithful believers will have their works judged and rewarded. The *judgment of the nations* takes place at the end of the Tribulation, when Christ has destroyed the armies of the world that attempted to destroy Israel (Revelation 19:11–21). The *Great White Throne Judgment* happens at the end of the Millennium. This is a judgment of unrepentant sinners; there are no rewards.

Julia Ward Howe described the scene when she wrote these words in the "Battle Hymn of the Republic":

He is sifting out the hearts of men before His
  judgment-seat;
Oh, be swift, my soul, to answer Him! Be jubi-
  lant, my feet!
Our God is marching on.

At the Great White Throne Judgment, unbelievers stand before God to give an account for their sins.
Because they have not trusted in Christ—because
they've rejected Him and His forgiveness—they cannot trust in His righteousness to cover them. They must
take responsibility for every single ungodly and unrigh-
teous thought, word, or deed. They are found guilty and
sentenced to death in the lake of fire.

Here we find both a foundation for forgiveness and
a hope for justice.

It may seem that the wicked enjoy unfettered privilege and unrestrained license (Psalm 73:3–18). In this
life, they may not appear to suffer any negative consequences for their behavior. On the contrary, sometimes
they seem to thrive and flourish—while we're the ones
who suffer! These people may have abused or mistreated
us, wronged or cheated us, yet it seems they easily escape
punishment.

But this reminder of future judgment in Revelation
can help us surrender thoughts of vengeance, hatred, or
unforgiveness here and now.

DR. DAVID JEREMIAH

The time is coming when justice will finally be served. On that day, in front of His white throne, God the Holy Judge will settle the accounts of those who have rebelled against His righteous ways. In His court there will be truth and justice—and eternal consequences for those who have stubbornly refused His mercy and grace. There will be no escape, no last-minute pardons or appeals. The punishment will literally be hell.

Lord, You are the Righteous Judge of all the earth. Vengeance is Yours, and so is the victory! Thank You for rescuing me from the judgment of the wicked that is to come. Help me be quick to hear Your voice and seek Your face as I live in the light of Your mercy and grace.

Read Revelation 20:11–15 in *The Jeremiah Study Bible.*

REVELATION 21:1–3

Then I saw "a new heaven and a new earth," for the first heaven and the first earth had passed away, and there was no longer any sea. I saw the Holy City, the new Jerusalem, coming down out of heaven from God, prepared as a bride beautifully dressed for her husband. And I heard a loud voice from the throne saying, "Look! God's dwelling place is now among the people, and he will dwell with them. They will be his people, and God himself will be with them and be their God."

53

NO FEAR

(Revelation 21:1–4)

We have come now to the part of the book of Revelation where the heavy cloud of judgment is lifted and we get a glimpse of the glorious inheritance that awaits us as children of the most High God. Revelation 21 is filled with good news for God's people! We have so much to look forward to in the new heaven and the new earth.

John had witnessed so much tragedy and triumph in his vision that it must have been overwhelming to see it all come to an end in blazing color. He writes, "Then I saw 'a new heaven and a new earth,' for the first heaven and the first earth had passed away, and there was no longer any sea. . . . He who was seated on the throne said, 'I am making everything new!'" (21:1, 5).

The new Jerusalem descends from heaven, revealing that believers' final destiny is not "up in heaven somewhere" but on *earth*—the new earth. But this new earth will never be plagued by the powers of evil, sin, death, or Satan.

John tells us that the new earth in his vision has no sea. It's hard to imagine a planet with no oceans. It seems strange that the new heaven and new earth will be without seas—especially to those of us who love the water or the beach! But John is writing symbolically here. We know that oceans separate people, so perhaps what he means is that we'll share one unified land, one continent. John had known the loneliness of isolation on the island of Patmos, separated by the Aegean Sea from all his loved ones and his church ministry on the mainland.

The sea also held all kinds of significance to ancient readers. To them, the sea was a raging, threatening, and fearful place—deep, dark, and unknown. Unpredictable. It represented chaos, disorder, and evil. In Revelation, the sea is the home of the dead (20:13) and is associated with the Abyss—the place from which the beast comes (11:7; 13:1).

So when John says there will be no more sea in the new heaven and earth, he is saying that there will be nothing to harm God's people or give them cause to fear.

Imagine that: no fear.

No fear of anything . . . ever again.

The tabernacle of God—His dwelling place —will now be among us on the new earth. We will live in the light of His love and His glorious presence, day after day after day.

And with that, the promise God made to Abraham, that all nations would be blessed in Him, is fulfilled (Genesis 18:18).

Lord God, thank You for the light of Your love and the warmth of Your presence. Fill me with Your Spirit, Your truth, and Your wisdom. Empower me to be a faithful minister of Your gospel, and guide me on Your path. Bring me safely home at the close of this day. In Jesus's name, Amen.

Read Revelation 21:1–4 in *The Jeremiah Study Bible*.

REVELATION 21:4

"'He will wipe every tear from their eyes. There will be no more death' or mourning or crying or pain, for the old order of things has passed away."

54

NO MORE TEARS
(Revelation 21:4)

The psalmist says God lists our tears on His scroll (Psalm 56:8). God sees our sadness and cares deeply. But in Revelation 21:4, John says that God "will wipe every tear" from our eyes. It's important to note that these aren't tears of shame or guilt, which are long gone at this point. These are the tears caused by all the hardship, persecution, pain, and death that His people have suffered on this earth.

In our eternal home, there will be no more sadness, no more tears. This is the end of all sorrow and suffering, the end of death. The curse of Genesis 3 will be completely broken and reversed. All the evils present in the old creation will be destroyed with the destruction of the old heaven and earth (21:1).

There will be nothing to mar our perfect relationship with Jesus and with each other. There will be no more sin—no arguments, no hurt feelings, no betrayal, no backsliding, or no bitter grudge-bearing. There will be no jealousy, anger, or wounded pride, no murder or crime, no corruption, or pollution.

There will be no injury, sickness, or disease. People who have been confined to wheelchairs will be able to walk freely. Those who have been blind will now be able to see the new earth in all its beauty. And the deaf will get to hear the heavenly choirs singing. The sick will be made well, and the wounded will be made whole. In our forever home, there will be no painful farewells; we will never again be separated from our loved ones.

The new earth will be filled with righteousness, peace, and joy. "Better is one day in your courts than a thousand elsewhere" (Psalm 84:10).

It's sad that so many people today—even many of God's people—live in continual bondage to the fear of death (Hebrews 2:14–15). There's no reason for believers to dread what lies ahead.

> The sting of death is sin. . . . But thanks be to God! He gives us the victory through our Lord Jesus Christ. (1 Corinthians 15:56–57)

Jesus has won the victory over sin, hell, and the grave. It's a victory He shares with all who believe— all who are willing to receive it, by receiving Him.

When we truly understand the glory of the place God has prepared for those who love Him, we need never fear again (1 Corinthians 2:9–10).

God, I can hardly imagine a world so wonderful—a place with no more tears of sadness, no more pain or sorrow or death. Help it become more real to me; fill me with longing for my eternal home. And give me a passion to reach those who have yet to hear the hope of the gospel, Your mercy and grace and the promise of eternal life—an eternal home in heaven with You!

Read Revelation 21:4 in *The Jeremiah Study Bible.*

REVELATION 21:5

He who was seated on the throne said, "I am making everything new!" Then he said, "Write this down, for these words are trustworthy and true."

55

THE ULTIMATE
EXTREME MAKEOVER
(Revelation 21:5–8)

For the first time since the very beginning, God speaks directly to John and to us: "I am making everything new!" (21:5). The creation of a new heaven and new earth is the climax of the book of Revelation. It's what the people of God have been longing for and looking forward to, through the ages, through all the challenges and trials of this life.

Hebrews 11:8–10 tells us:

> By faith Abraham, when called to go to a place he would later receive as his inheritance, obeyed and went, even though he did not know where he was going. By faith he made his home in the promised land like a stranger in a foreign country; he lived in tents, as did Isaac and Jacob, who were heirs with him of the same promise. For he was looking forward to the city with foundations, whose architect and builder is God.

According to this same chapter, Moses and all the

other great heroes of the faith were looking ahead to their reward. "They were longing for a better country—a heavenly one. Therefore God is not ashamed to be called their God, for he has prepared a city for them" (Hebrews 11:16).

It won't be long now!

No one knows for sure exactly how God will bring the new heaven and earth into existence. Some people refer to 2 Peter 3:10–12 and suggest that God is going to blow up the planet and start over. But I believe God is going to remake, renew, refresh, and refurbish the existing heaven and earth. Somehow, through a holy, purifying fire, every evil and polluted thing will be cleansed from the planet.

Just as we can clean something old so that it becomes "new" again, so I believe God will cleanse the earth and make it the brand-new heaven and earth in which we will dwell for eternity.

Jesus tells us He is the "Alpha and the Omega"—the Greek alphabet equivalent of "A to Z." It's an expression indicating God's absolute sovereignty over all things (Revelation 1:8). He is the Beginner of the beginning and the Ender of the end. In Genesis, He stands at the beginning of creation (Genesis 1–2) and now He stands at the end in a new creation (Revelation 21–22).

He is faithful to keep every promise to His people and to fulfill every Word. "Those who are victorious will inherit all this, and I will be their God and they will be my children" (21:7).

As children of the King of kings and Lord of lords, we are rightful heirs to all the promises of God in the Davidic Covenant. We will have the privileges of rule and intimacy with the Father (2 Samuel 7:12–14).

What a wonderful promise! What a precious hope! Oh, the joy that awaits us on that day when we finally see Jesus face-to-face and enter into His glorious presence forever.

Therefore we do not lose heart. Though outwardly we are wasting away, yet inwardly we are being renewed day by day. For our light and momentary troubles are achieving for us an eternal glory that far outweighs them all. So we fix our eyes not on what is seen, but on what is unseen, since what is seen is temporary, but what is unseen is eternal. (2 Corinthians 4:16–18)

Creator of heaven and earth, how grateful I am that someday You will make all things new— including me! How I look forward to that day.

Read Revelation 21:5–8 in *The Jeremiah Study Bible.*

REVELATION 21:9–11, 25–27

One of the seven angels who had the seven bowls full of the seven last plagues came and said to me, "Come, I will show you the bride, the wife of the Lamb." And he carried me away in the Spirit to a mountain great and high, and showed me the Holy City, Jerusalem, coming down out of heaven from God. It shone with the glory of God, and its brilliance was like that of a very precious jewel, like a jasper, clear as crystal. . . .

On no day will its gates ever be shut, for there will be no night there. The glory and honor of the nations will be brought into it. Nothing impure will ever enter it, nor will anyone who does what is shameful or deceitful, but only those whose names are written in the Lamb's book of life.

56

THERE'S NO PLACE LIKE HOME

(Revelation 21:9–27)

Almost since time began, human beings have speculated about what awaits us in the world to come. It's hard to even imagine all the wonders that will be ours to explore. The Bible tells us in 1 Corinthians 2:9–10:

"What no eye has seen,
    what no ear has heard,
and what no human mind has conceived"—
    the things God has prepared for those who
    love him—
these are the things God has revealed to us by
his Spirit.

In Revelation 21:1–22:5, we catch glimpses of this glorious future God has in store for us. We learn that we'll live and reign with Christ in a beautiful city called the New Jerusalem.

Here's what else we learn about our future home:

The city will come down to us on earth. John sees the new Jerusalem *descending*, dispelling the notion that our eternal home is vaguely "up there in heaven" somewhere (21:1–3).

It is free from the curse, free of sin and death, free of evil and evil people. In the new Jerusalem, "the old order of things has passed away" (21:4). This includes all sin and its awful consequences.

It is a place of indescribable beauty. Some of the traditional images of heaven—such as pearly gates and streets of gold—have their origin in John's attempt to put into words the stunning, unspeakable glory of the vision he was given (21:18–21).

It is a city of giant proportions. The new Jerusalem has room for people redeemed from every tribe, tongue, and nation throughout all history. Each dimension is approximately 1,400 miles, making the base 1,960,000 square miles! The ground floor alone would provide enough space for more people than have ever lived in the history of the world.

It is a godly city. The entire city will be a holy temple where God and the Lamb dwell and whose inhabitants will all be "priests"—people in the service of God. Because there is no fear of attack, the gates are never closed. All the nations of the earth are free to come and go as they please.

It is a city of life. A river of life flows from God's throne, watering trees that bear food for the inhabitants—as it was in the beginning (22:1–2). God's servants will have life-giving, meaningful work to do (22:3). And they will rule with Jesus over the new creation forever (22:5).

It is home. Sometimes heaven is referred to as a country, and we think of its vastness. Sometimes heaven is called a kingdom, and we think of its orderliness. Sometimes heaven is called Paradise, and we imagine its beauty. Sometimes heaven is referred to as a city, and we think of its citizens. But when we call heaven the Father's house, we think of intimacy—the closeness we will share with Him and with all who are part of this one big, happy family!

Lord Jesus, help me remember that I'm a pilgrim in this world and that my true home is in heaven. How I long for the day when I'll see You face-to-face and live in the light of Your glorious presence forever!

Read Revelation 21:9–27 in *The Jeremiah Study Bible.*

REVELATION 22:1–2

Then the angel showed me the river of the water of life, as clear as crystal, flowing from the throne of God and of the Lamb down the middle of the great street of the city. On each side of the river stood the tree of life, bearing twelve crops of fruit, yielding its fruit every month. And the leaves of the tree are for the healing of the nations.

57

FAR AS THE CURSE
IS FOUND

(Revelation 22:1–2)

E ver since Adam and Eve sinned in the Garden of Eden, the earth and its inhabitants have been laboring under a dreadful curse (Genesis 3:14–19). And subsequently, we have desperately longed to be free of this curse and its painful consequences.

In Genesis 3:15, God promised,

> I will put enmity
> between you and the woman,
>   and between your offspring and hers;
> he will crush your head,
>   and you will strike his heel.

Bible scholars call this verse the *protoevangelium* (*proto* means "first"; *evangelium* means "gospel" or good news) because the words "he will crush your head, and you will strike his heel" contain the seed form of the earliest statement of the "first gospel"—the good news of salvation. The coming of the woman's offspring was fulfilled in Jesus's birth (Galatians 4:4). On the cross, Jesus's body was bruised and broken; at the Second Coming of

Christ, Satan's head will be crushed (Romans 16:20).

The apostle Paul points out that the longing for deliverance is something that even the natural world experiences:

> For the creation was subjected to frustration, not by its own choice, but by the will of the one who subjected it, in hope that the creation itself will be liberated from its bondage to decay and brought into the freedom and glory of the children of God.
>
> We know that the whole creation has been groaning as in the pains of childbirth right up to the present time. Not only so, but we ourselves, who have the firstfruits of the Spirit, groan inwardly as we wait eagerly for our adoption to sonship, the redemption of our bodies. For in this hope we were saved. (Romans 8:20–24)

In last chapter of the Bible, we finally see the long-awaited fulfillment of God's promise: "No longer will there be any curse" (Revelation 22:3).

The new creation will be a return to the Garden of Eden; Paradise lost is now Paradise regained! God's original order will be restored, with the redeemed ruling over all creation with Christ.

In Paradise, the river of life flows down through the

middle of the city, and the tree of life—once guarded by a cherubim with a flaming sword in Eden—reappears to beckon the weary pilgrims of the Lord to their future inheritance. The tree of life, which was taken away in the Garden of Eden, is restored. This magnificent tree is laden with fruit, and we are told there is a different crop every month. "And the leaves of the tree are for the healing of the nations" (22:2).

In the words of hymn writer Isaac Watts:

No more let sin and sorrow grow
Nor thorns infest the ground;
He comes to make his blessings flow
Far as the curse is found.

Joy to the world, indeed!

Heavenly Father, I join with the creation in longing for the curse on the earth to be lifted, but I long even more for the joy that is to come when You take Your rightful place as King and rule this world with truth and grace! Even now, help me prepare room in my heart for You.

Read Revelation 22:1–2 in *The Jeremiah Study Bible.*

REVELATION 22:3–5

No longer will there be any curse. The throne of God and of the Lamb will be in the city, and his servants will serve him. They will see his face, and his name will be on their foreheads. There will be no more night. They will not need the light of a lamp or the light of the sun, for the Lord God will give them light. And they will reign for ever and ever.

58

WHAT WILL WE DO IN HEAVEN?

(Revelation 22:3–6)

Contrary to the way it's often depicted in commercials and TV shows, heaven isn't a place where "good" people are bored out of their minds, floating sleepily along on puffy white clouds and yawning in-between harp solos. Nothing could be further from the truth!

So what will we do forever and ever in heaven? How will we spend eternity? The Bible tells us more about it than we might think.

For one thing, *we will sing* (19:1–8). Heaven is not one never-ending church service, as some well-meaning believers have suggested. But there will be a lot of joyful singing, a lot of celebrating. Revelation contains more songs than any other book of the Bible except Psalms.

No doubt many well-known passages in the Psalms that speak of the passionate worship of God will be fulfilled in those days. And it will be bliss! We may stumble through the songs we try to sing here on earth, but we'll sound beautiful in heaven. Imagine joining the choirs of thousands, or perhaps millions, all with access to perfect instruments to play. Honestly, we can't even begin to comprehend how glorious this music will be!

We will serve (22:3, 6). We'll function as servants of God in the truest sense. We'll be given meaningful and fulfilling work to do—the kind that energizes us, the kind that perfectly suits our individual gifts and talents, the kind that brings us great reward. We will do tasks happily, without weariness, because we have found our purpose. We will be living out our high and holy calling. And we will love every eternal minute of it.

We will share. Heaven will be the ultimate experience of fellowship—rich, meaningful connection with others, community in its purest form. No more generation gap or cross-cultural confusion. No socioeconomic differences, no prejudice or hate. We'll be able to meet the great men and women of past generations, as well as those in the Bible. We can spend quality time with the apostles John and Paul and Peter, or we can talk to Daniel and David and Ruth and Esther. We'll also have the opportunity to meet and fellowship with countless other believers we have never met.

And of course, all of our Christian friends and family members who have gone before us will be there too. How wonderful it will be to see our loved ones again and talk with the parents, children, other relatives, and friends we have lost during our earthly lives. What a joy to realize that each day we live brings us closer to seeing them again! The years of grief, loneliness, and pain we have experienced without those we love will be erased. We will have forever to love them and be loved by them in return.

Most important of all . . .

We will savor unbroken and joyous fellowship with the Father, Son, and Spirit, reigning with Christ, the King of kings and Lord of lords forever and ever (22:5)!

Hallelujah!

Lord God, even now I will sing Your praises, serve You faithfully, share in community, and savor Your presence—all in eager anticipation of the day when I will sing, serve, share, and savor for all eternity!

Read Revelation 22:3–6 in *The Jeremiah Study Bible*.

REVELATION 22:7, 10–13

"Look, I am coming soon! Blessed is the one who keeps the words of the prophecy written in this scroll." . . .

Then he told me, "Do not seal up the words of the prophecy of this scroll, because the time is near. Let the one who does wrong continue to do wrong; let the vile person continue to be vile; let the one who does right continue to do right; and let the holy person continue to be holy."

"Look, I am coming soon! My reward is with me, and I will give to each person according to what they have done. I am the Alpha and the Omega, the First and the Last, the Beginning and the End."

59

WHAT SHOULD
WE DO UNTIL THEN?

(Revelation 22:7–16)

How should we live until the Rapture of the Church takes place or until we each see Jesus face-to-face? How should we live as the things prophesied in the book of Revelation begin to unfold?

First, we should *walk submissively*. The angel tells John that he should "keep" the things he has been shown (22:7). The word *keep* (Greek *tereo*) literally means "to walk under the authority of." In essence, this verse gives us a blessing: "Blessed is the one who walks submissively under the authority of God's Word until Jesus returns." What does it mean to "keep" God's Word? It doesn't mean to just buy a Bible and keep it on your shelf. It means to read it, study it, believe it, and obey it. We must allow the Word not only to inform us but to trans-form our thinking and direct our daily lives.

Second, we should *worship triumphantly*. When John hears that Jesus is coming quickly, he falls down in worship. In fact, John's consistent response to news about prophetic events is to worship—and ours should be too.

Third, we should *witness urgently*. John is told not to seal up the prophecy "because the time is near" (22:10). The revelation he received needs to be shared. Prophecy is one of the most effective tools we have for persuading people to come to Christ (2 Corinthians 5:11). Indeed, anyone who can read about the future days of Tribulation on earth and not be motivated to tell others how to escape the coming wrath of God has not truly been touched by the words of this prophecy.

Fourth, we should *work fervently*. "Look, I am coming soon! My reward is with me, and I will give to each person according to what they have done" (Revelation 22:12). It's important to remember that we will all stand before the Judgment Seat of Christ. Believers, however, are not judged according to their salvation but are given their rewards for faithfulness and good works. Again, as Christians, we can't lose our salvation, but it is possible to lose our rewards. This should motivate us to work fervently for the Lord. We only have a short time on this earth in which to serve Him, so whatever we could or should do for Him—whatever He has called us to do—we need to do now!

Finally, we are to *watch expectantly*. Three times in Revelation 22, the swift coming of the Lord Jesus is emphasized (22:7, 12, 20). When the Lord comes for His own, He will come with the speed of lightning!

Now is the time to prepare for His coming; now is the time to open our eyes and begin watching expectantly for His return. Now is the time to do all we can, by His strength and for His glory, before it is too late.

Jesus, I realize the days are short and time is precious. I have just a little while to love You and serve You here on earth. Help me to live this day in light of eternity. Whatever I should do for You today, empower me to do it now!

Read Revelation 22:7–16 in *The Jeremiah Study Bible*.

REVELATION 22:17–21

The Spirit and the bride say, "Come!" And let the one who hears say, "Come!" Let the one who is thirsty come; and let the one who wishes take the free gift of the water of life.

I warn everyone who hears the words of the prophecy of this scroll: If anyone adds anything to them, God will add to that person the plagues described in this scroll. And if anyone takes words away from this scroll of prophecy, God will take away from that person any share in the tree of life and in the Holy City, which are described in this scroll.

He who testifies to these things says, "Yes, I am coming soon."

Amen. Come, Lord Jesus.

The grace of the Lord Jesus be with God's people. Amen.

60

A SPECIAL INVITATION FOR YOU

(Revelation 22:17–21)

It would be heartbreaking to read Revelation, glimpse the future through John's visions, and then leave this book without ever personally coming to know the One who is to come. And so we find this final invitation: "The Spirit and the bride say, 'Come!' And let the one who hears say, 'Come!' Let the one who is thirsty come; and let the one who wishes take the free gift of the water of life" (22:17).

The first part of the verse is an invitation for Christ to come back to the world. The last part of the verse is an invitation for the world to come back to Christ.

Why do we respond to the invitation to come to Christ? It's because we're thirsty, because everything else in life seems dry and empty.

How do we respond? Well, we don't come to Christ by intellect alone, or even with the heart alone. We come to Christ because we *decide* to do so. It's a matter of the will.

God wants us to accept His precious gift—the gift of His Son, Jesus Christ, who died on the cross that we might be saved. He wants us to have eternal life with Him in the new heaven and the new earth. He makes it really simple.

This presentation of the gospel is about as pure and uncomplicated as it gets: Are you thirsty? Then come and drink the living water.

You don't have to earn your salvation. You just have to take the free gift. Choose to receive it!

> Repent, then, and turn to God, so that your sins may be wiped out, that times of refreshing may come from the Lord. (Acts 3:19)

Just as the book of Revelation began, so it ends—with an invitation and a blessing for those who hear and obey God's Word (Revelation 1:3; 22:7). Here, however, there is also a curse. John was commissioned to write these words, and anyone who tampers with them will bear the consequences of judgment from God. It's an important reminder. We haven't been asked to edit or to rewrite the invitation; we've only been asked to RSVP.

Then the Lord Jesus puts His own signature at the end. He says, "Yes, I am coming soon"—and all His followers respond, "Amen. Come, Lord Jesus" (22:20).

The closing benediction brings us back to the message of the gospel, the gift of His grace (22:21).

Sometimes we get so caught up in our plans, we forget that the very best thing that could happen to us if we are believers is for the Lord Jesus Christ to return today. But anyone who has their spiritual priorities in place will find themselves longing for His return.

What about you? Is your heart's cry, "Come, Lord Jesus"?

Help me respond wholeheartedly to Your invitation and freely receive the gift of Your grace. Teach me how to live in the light of eternity today. With all that I am, I worship You, and join in the chorus of faith, crying, "Amen. Come, Lord Jesus!"

Read Revelation 22:17–21 in *The Jeremiah Study Bible*.

ABOUT THE AUTHOR

DR. DAVID JEREMIAH is the senior pastor of Shadow Mountain Community Church in El Cajon, California. Messages preached in the pulpit at Shadow Mountain form the basis of *Turning Point*, his international broadcast ministry. The outreach of Turning Point Radio and Television programs is now worldwide. *Momento Decisivo*, the Spanish edition of *Turning Point*, is heard in every country that has a Spanish-speaking population. Thousands of responses to these ministries are received every day from people all over the world.

Dr. Jeremiah has authored more than fifty books, including *A Life Beyond Amazing: Nine Decisions That Will Transform Your Life Today*, *Is This the End?*, *Agents of Babylon*, *Agents of the Apocalypse*, *God Loves You: He Always Has—He Always Will*, *I Never Thought I'd See the Day*, *The Coming Armageddon*, and *What in the World Is Going On?* In 2013, Dr. Jeremiah published *The Jeremiah Study Bible*, a comprehensive yet easy-to-understand version that was over forty years in the making.

Dr. Jeremiah is a much in demand as a speaker because of his commitment to the truth of the Bible and his special ability to help people understand how to apply biblical principles to everyday living. Dr. and Mrs. Jeremiah are parents of four children and grandparents of twelve.

IF YOU ENJOYED THIS BOOK, WILL YOU CONSIDER SHARING THE MESSAGE WITH OTHERS?

Mention the book in a blog post or through Facebook, Twitter, or upload a picture through Instagram.

Recommend this book to those in your small group, book club, workplace, and classes.

Head over to facebook.com/worthypublishing, "LIKE" the page, and post a comment about what you enjoyed the most.

Tweet "I recommend reading #WhenChristAppears by @Dr. David Jeremiah // @worthypub"

Pick up a copy for someone you know who would be challenged and encouraged by this message.

Write a book review online.

WORTHY®
PUBLISHING

Visit us at worthypublishing.com

twitter.com/worthypub

youtube.com/worthypublishing

facebook.com/worthypublishing

instagram.com/worthypub